CHRIS M. CONRAD

LIKE A BLIND MAN RUNNING

AN INVITATION TO A
RENEWED LIFE IN CHRIST

TRILOGY
A WHOLLY OWNED SUBSIDIARY OF TBN
PROFESSIONAL PUBLISHING MEETS POWERFUL PROMOTION

Like a Blind Man Running
Trilogy Christian Publishers
A Wholly Owned Subsidiary of Trinity Broadcasting Network
2442 Michelle Drive
Tustin, CA 92780

Copyright © 2024 by Chris M. Conrad

Scripture quotations marked ESV are taken from the ESV® Bible (The Holy Bible, English Standard Version®), copyright © 2001 by Crossway Bibles, a publishing ministry of Good News Publishers. Used by permission. All rights reserved.

Scripture quotations marked NKJV are taken from the New King James Version®. Copyright © 1982 by Thomas Nelson. Used by permission. All rights reserved.

All rights reserved, including the right to reproduce this book or portions thereof in any form whatsoever.

For information, address Trilogy Christian Publishing
Rights Department, 2442 Michelle Drive, Tustin, Ca 92780.

Trilogy Christian Publishing/ TBN and colophon are trademarks of Trinity Broadcasting Network.

For information about special discounts for bulk purchases, please contact Trilogy Christian Publishing.

Trilogy Disclaimer: The views and content expressed in this book are those of the author and may not necessarily reflect the views and doctrine of Trilogy Christian Publishing or the Trinity Broadcasting Network.

10 9 8 7 6 5 4 3 2 1
Library of Congress Cataloging-in-Publication Data is available.
ISBN 979-8-89333-247-6
ISBN 979-8-89333-248-3 (ebook)

DEDICATION

To Teresa, my daughter and my muse. You challenge me to risk and inspire me to leap.

To Frank Tillapaugh, who years ago challenged me to this task. You saw in me what I could not envision in myself. At last, I'm trusting your insight and answering God's call.

To my wife, Vickie, and daughter Heather, and all those, like Karin and Katie, Tom and Monica, and Ron, who have helped me dream, encouraged me, helped edit, and covered me in prayer.

Thank you.

TABLE OF CONTENTS

INTRODUCTION 9
   Come On In, Let's Sit and Talk 9
   You Are Invited 14

CHAPTER 1: YEARNING 18
   Limited 18
   Yearning 21
   Reckless 23

CHAPTER 2: LABEL 27
   A Dissatisfied People 27
   A Common Story 29
   Sidelined 30

CHAPTER 3: COLLISION 39
   Collision Course 39
   Destroying Barriers 43
   Divine Collisions 46
   Choices 48

CHAPTER 4: QUESTIONS AND DECISIONS 50
   Where Is Your God? 50
   The Exchange 53
   What Would You Do? 55

CHAPTER 5: BREAKTHROUGH 59
   Desperate 59

Breakthrough 61
CHAPTER 6: RECOVERY 69
    Thieves 69
    Throttled Trust 71
    Unworthiness 73
    Emptiness 74
    Anger/Bitterness 76
    Cynicism/Control 77
    Desire 78
    Recovery 80
CHAPTER 7: CLARITY 84
    Conflict 84
    Renewed 86
    The Tension of In-Between 89
    Acceptance 91
CHAPTER 8: FOLLOW 92
    Invitation 92
    Personhood 97
    Palms Down 99
    The Tenacious Voice 100
    Follow 102
CHAPTER 9: GRACE AND GRIEF 104
    Grace and Grief 104
    The Sacrament of the Road 106

- TABLE OF CONTENTS -

CHAPTER 10: EXPECTATIONS 111
    Expectations Are Powerful 111
    Expect Trials, Troubles, and Temptations 113
    Expect Mercy and Grace 117
    Expect to Encounter God Almighty 119
    Expect Worship to Be Your New Normal 120
    Expect an Eternal Reward 122
    Expect More of Him, Less of You 123
EPILOGUE: TRAVELING ON YOUR JERICHO ROAD 124
    Entering in Hope: Hold Tightly to Hope 125
    Desire 127
    Traveling On, or Disciplines for the Inner Life
    Prayer: Breathing Out 129
    Step One 132
    Step Two 132
    Step Three 132
    Quiet Reflection: Breathing In 133
    Read for Transformation 135
    Fasting: Humbling Yourself Before the Lord 136
    Finding Your Stride 137
A CLOSING PRAYER 140
ABOUT THE AUTHOR 141
BIBLIOGRAPHY 143
REFERENCES 146

INTRODUCTION

COME ON IN, LET'S SIT AND TALK

"Come on in!" "Dinner starts at six, why don't you come early?" "Let's meet for coffee or lunch." Oh, how I love words like these spoken to me! I get excited about each invitation I receive, and you should know that it is hard for me to say no to most invitations. We should all be captured by what invitations mean because they are all about being chosen to share a special moment with someone. I love to get invitations, but I really love to hand out invitations, too. It makes my life feel complete to include someone special in a meaningful activity. I don't know about you, but I thoroughly love one-on-one moments. Things like camping or having dinner out with my wife, hiking with my daughter or closest friend, or going on a hunting trip with my son-in-law. One of my favorite activities is to invite one of my two daughters or four granddaughters out to eat. It's just me and one of "my girls" enjoying good food and good conversation. Life just doesn't get much better than that. Except, perhaps, when I am on the receiving end of an invitation…that is a remarkable thing, my friend, because invitations are about connecting with another person. I am always a bit surprised when someone wants to include me in a special moment with them. It is humbling and exhilarating at the same time. Man, oh man. I love invitations! The next time you receive a dinner, a movie, a wedding invitation, or anything else, you need to pause for just a moment to notice just how that feels because invitations are remarkably special moments. Every invitation should be celebrated, so celebrate because you have been chosen!

Just this morning, I invited granddaughter number three out to breakfast. We had such a good time, sharing good food and remembering some things about our lives that had grown cold and faded in memory. I reminded "number three" that we can get so used to having someone in our life that we can grow complacent, forgetting those things that bind us to each other. She is learning that choosing to nurture a relationship is just one more form of invitation.

I would say that the most significant invitation I have ever given was the night I proposed to my wife. She said "yes," and because she accepted that proposal, we have shared more than fifty years of laughter, sadness, trials, blessings, and adventures.

If I asked you to tell me about the most significant invitation you have received, would you be able to tell me about it? As someone who works with families finding their way through grief and loss, I often ask thought-provoking questions like this. Most of the time, people are unable to answer questions like this because it is a question that is not often considered. But it should be. I'll ask again: tell me about the most significant invitation you have ever received. Was it to a wedding? How about a graduation or the dedication or adoption of a child? What was it about that invitation that was so significant for you? Right now, I wish we were sitting together so I could hear you tell me about that invitation!

I still remember the most significant invitation I have ever received, and you should know that I have been invited to weddings, parties, graduations, and all manner of child dedications. I have been invited on cruises and hunting trips. I have often been invited to preach at a church or retreat, and I have been invited to work with some very remarkable people who have changed the trajectory of my life. But of all the invitations I have received, the one that stands out above them all was given to me when I was very young. In a basement classroom of a church in central Ohio, my second-grade Sunday school teacher invited me and others to surrender our lives to Jesus Christ; I did that Sunday. I said yes to an invitation that has set me on a new trajectory that continues to this day. I wish I could say that

I have been steadily on track since that day, but I cannot. There have been seasons of questions, seasons of full-on rebellion, and seasons of renewal, but taken together, they have moved me closer to Jesus' heart. Every season that has not been toward Him but away from Him has caused some damage. But these seasons have also increased my hunger for greater intimacy with Him.

I wonder if the same could be said for you. Is there a noise in your spirit that you cannot seem to identify? You may have a deep-down feeling that things are not quite right, but you are just not sure what name to give it; it's there just below the surface, gnawing away at your spirit, hidden in the shadows. Because it lurks in the shadows and can easily disguise itself, most of the time, you just dismiss that gnawing feeling in your heart. It's not large or overbearing. It does not scream for your attention. If anything, it faintly whispers to you when your world finally quiets down. "Just what is that?" you ask yourself. Could this disquiet in your soul be an invitation to increase your hunger for greater intimacy with your Creator and Savior? Perhaps your heart is longing for its Maker and Savior while your unidentified gnawing is being used to move you from your place of brokenness and isolation toward healing and intimacy with Jesus. For some of you, your story may be a bit different; you may be reading this because you responded to that invitation from Jesus earlier in life, but you have gotten so far off track that you are not sure that you can ever find your way back to spiritual healing and peace. Perhaps you may be one of the lucky ones who have identified that disquiet bouncing around in your spirit. You know what you are dealing with, and while it is uncomfortable and, at times, intrusive, you have been able to manage it so far. So, even though you know your brokenness full well, you push it to the periphery of your life, thinking that you can deal with it some other, more convenient time. But, have you noticed that the more you delay in dealing with it, the easier it is to put off honestly and finally put your turmoil to rest?

Honestly, this happens to everyone! Check scripture. Everyone who was pursuing a real relationship with God had a moment when they doubted, questioned, or ran away from Him. David had more than one of these seasons. Paul wrote to the Philippians: *"For to me to live is Christ, and to die is gain. If I am to live in the flesh, that means fruitful labor for me. Yet which I shall choose I cannot tell. I am hard-pressed between the two. My desire is to depart and be with Christ, for that is far better."*[1] Habakkuk wrestled with and questioned God, Jeremiah cried out to God, and Peter failed more than once. And, of course, Thomas doubted without concrete proof, while Jonah ran away because he did not believe that anyone outside his circle of fellowship was qualified to know God. Everyone has a season or two that move us from a centered relationship with God into a season in which we doubt, question, or drift. There are seasons of overt sin and seasons of control over temptations, but even then, we can feel victory is small and temporary; we feel like we lack depth of spirit. This book is written by one who understands the need to be invited to come close to Jesus. You will notice how personal this book feels. That is because I have had seasons of victory, other seasons defined by feelings of unworthiness, and still others of outright rebellion. But His mercies are new every morning, and He continues to offer invitations to be healed of all the dysfunction that seems to be so at home in my soul.

YOU ARE INVITED

Invitations are found throughout the Scriptures, from the opening pages, where God invited Adam and Eve to walk and talk daily, to the closing pages, where God invites all His saints to the marriage supper of the Lamb. He invited Moses into a face-to-face relationship, and later on in history, He invited King

- INTRODUCTION -

David to repent of his sin, and David found just what he needed: a renewed joy in his salvation and a God willing to continue to uphold him.[2] Then, when the Word became flesh[3], He invited everyone who would listen into the kingdom of God. He healed, and He restored, and His invitations are still being handed out today.

What makes God's invitations so significant is that He is inviting us out of our brokenness and ceaseless striving into life that is healed and filled with His presence. He invites us to find fulfillment through His grace and mercy as He provides what we cannot possibly provide for ourselves!

> Ho! Everyone who thirsts, come to the waters; and you who have no money, come, buy and eat. Yes, come, buy wine and milk without money and without price. Why do you spend money for what is not bread, and your wages for what does not satisfy? Listen carefully to Me, and eat what is good, and let your soul delight itself in abundance. Incline your ear, and come to Me. Hear, and your soul shall live; and I will make an everlasting covenant with you—the sure mercies of David.[4]

Through the Prophet Isaiah, God asks us why we are working so hard to provide our healing and why we are so feverously pursuing that which does not satisfy us. In our search for abundance, we can grab some things that look so good and satisfying but eventually drain us, and then, as they abandon us, we are stranded in another season of searching and longing. Why do we live like this? God has so much more waiting for us, but to find abundance, we must first respond to His invitation.

Perhaps the best-known biblical invitation is found in Luke chapter 11 when the father invites his wayward son back into the family. That parable is one that all of us need to review from time to time. There is a place for the wayward in His home and at His table. Oh, how I long for that home! Tell me, are you in need of being invited back to God's table?

Do you need to hear the Father's words of joy and invitation calling you back into His family? Were you once close, but now you feel so far from home?

I vividly remember those early days of faith in Jesus Christ. Do you? But I also have clear memories of seasons of drift, seasons of outright rebellion, and seasons of renewal when the freshness of life in Christ calmed all the storms that can so easily rage in me. This book is an invitation to find your way out of

- INTRODUCTION -

the darkness and back into the light. Together, we will examine the life of one very obscure biblical personality, how he found himself enslaved by a darkness that settled in on him for a very long time, and how one small invitation in a desperate moment transformed him physically and spiritually. As you read his story, you may be struck by how similar your story is to his. Take hope in that because if he could find what he needed in Jesus and have what he had lost restored, so can you. So, I invite you to come, sit with the scriptures, and sit with all your pain because that pain can open the door to desperation, which is the threshold to transformation.

Come on in, let's sit together for a while. You are invited to a renewed life in Christ.

CHAPTER 1: YEARNING

> "The (spiritual) organ of *experience* is Love, and the (spiritual) organ of *knowledge* is Faith."
>
> —A. W. Tozer

LIMITED

What you believe to be true about God will never be tested when you have your own resources. But everything you hope to be true about God will only be revealed when you are going through a hard time and have no resources. You know this to be true even if it is not something you have said out loud. "He is able" too easily rolls off the tongue, even while your heart and mind race to find your own solution to your desperate need. You and I have enough teaching and training to know that God is unlimited and that He is able to meet every need, no matter how impossible. Yet, how often have you pulled back in your trust? How often have you questioned how He is responding to your prayers? Trusting God and being fully surrendered to His will and direction for your life can be a scary and uncertain thing. He is, after all, known as a "dangerous God". If you are unsure about this "dangerous God" title, reread the account of Abraham and his only son, Isaac, or skip ahead in your Bible to the story of Daniel. God often tests the ones He loves, making Him a bit dangerous, don't you think? You know that He is for you, yet there are moments when you wonder if you can trust Him because of all that He has asked of you. I've seen it firsthand in others, and I have crumbled under the weight of testing as I hoped for a greater victory. We all want to see God move into our hopeless situation, and we have dreamt about His intervention that makes our dreams come true. Like a Hollywood movie, our hero, God, shows up at just the right time, in just the right way. He makes the sun shine all the brighter while every enemy is vanquished. He makes our every desire come true, and then the credits roll.

Truth be told, there are people, me included, who have experienced His miraculous intervention in the impossible valleys of life. I've seen actual healings and have been used as the instrument for some of those healings. I have been privileged to intercede for people who seemed to be beyond the touch of grace, but I have come to know God personally; then, I watched as their whole life has been transformed. Like you, I have prayed and prayed for something that still has not found its way into my life, even though I know God can answer that yet unanswered prayer.

But even though He is able and He has moved in our lives, there are so many influences that press in on us, working to steal what little hope and strength we do have. You may not have a debilitating disadvantage that some people struggle with daily, but if you are honest, there is also a part of your spiritual life that is more limited than you would like. There has been prayer after prayer, but still no intervention from the Lord Jesus. You may have asked how long you must wait for Him to intervene. So, you just settle in with what seems to be His indifference, living your life with some level of disappointment in how He has moved into your impossible need. This, in turn, breeds increased detachment in your spiritual life. Church and quiet time remain part of your life, but there is little spiritual power, and you have decided that this is normal Christian living, even though, deep down, you hope for more.

I have also seen it work like this for some people: their early days with the Lord are like a blazing sunrise. Those days are intense and beautiful. But those early days of beauty and intensity are somehow overcome by darkness and bitterness because of some personal expectation that was not met by the Lord. For some strange reason, it is a general trait of humanity to believe that God Almighty works for and serves us. Then, when He fails to live up to our standards, He is pushed out of sight. If that is you, please hold on. I know that you picked up this book while hoping for some answers to cure your current hopelessness. What you need to know is that everyone who has picked up this book has experienced some kind of spiritual setback. Many of us have had spiritual eyes to see, but something that should not have happened did. Now, our eyes are dimmer, if not fully blinded to spiritual things. We need new eyes, new ears, and a new heart. But how do we get there? What must we do? We can feel so limited, so held in place by our awkward spiritual state.

I wonder, do we need to be just a bit more desperate for His touch, His presence, His comforting words and embrace? What would happen to us if we dared to throw off all our expectations and demands? Would a heart desperate for Him position us nearer to Him so that He begins to overwhelm our needs?

YEARNING

How do you handle life when things just don't work out the way you expected? Does that unmet expectation rob you of a deeper yearning for Him, or does it just deepen your disappointment? Often, what happens to us is that after years of unanswered prayer, we lose our desperate hearts, and we begin to accept that this is the way things are supposed to be. How would you describe your yearning for Him? Are you able to honestly pray the words of the Sons of Korah: *"As the deer pants for the water brooks, so pants my soul for You, O God. My soul thirsts for God, for the living God...."*[5] I'm sure you have noticed that yearning is the track that moves us forward in all life's pursuits. Your journey has been long, and at times it seems darker than you would like. You still have some trust in what God can do, but you just don't know how to get Him to cooperate with your agenda. You want so much more in your relationship with Him, but it's been harder than you expected, and you now go through the motions, doing the Christian thing so that no one knows the actual questions you are wrestling with. Yearning is necessary in our spiritual life, just as it is in other pursuits, but it has been my experience and observation that spiritual yearning is not always met with open arms. Most often, we hold back in spiritual things because we fear spiritual excess more than we fear spiritual lack. So, we have convinced ourselves that it would be better to tame our spiritual yearnings than to become too extreme. I wonder if the age we live in has made us skeptical, or has it just made us tired? Are we cynics or just weary?

RECKLESS

I think it's a bit of both: we are weary with the weight of life and sin, which makes us more cynical than we should be. I'll bet there was a time in your life when you were more willing to embrace risk to have Him and His answer for your situation. I know that I have far more to lose now than I did when I was younger. Ironically, He has blessed me so much that it can be harder to trust Him with what He has given me. I'm not nearly as reckless in my trust in Him as I once was. So, I wonder, is that what the Spirit is addressing in Revelation 2:4? *"But I have this against you, that you have abandoned the love you had at first."* Is the loss of my first love actually a limited willingness to fully trust Him? Do I need to be more reckless in my trust? Have I limited what He is able to do in me and through me because I have pulled my trust into a safer place? The dictionary defines reckless as an act of someone who does something without thinking or caring about the consequences. I can't help but wonder, is the cure for our cynicism and weariness found in a heart renewed and desperate for Him? I often wonder if I need to be a bit more reckless in seeking Him and yearning for Him. Now, please don't misunderstand, I am an advocate of seeking God with your head as much as your heart. I'm not arguing for thoughtlessness but a reckless hunger that is unsatisfied with anything less than His presence and heart.

It is interesting to note that in Exodus chapter 33, Joshua could not tear himself away from the place that God had just visited. Here is what is written about Joshua's hunger for the presence of the Lord:

> And when all the people saw the pillar of cloud standing at the entrance of the tent, all the people would rise up and worship, each at his tent door. Thus the LORD used to speak to Moses face to face, as a man speaks to his friend. When Moses turned again into the camp, his assistant Joshua the son of Nun, a young man, would not depart from the tent.[6]

Clearly, Joshua's desire was for more than a simple answer to a prayer. Moses had departed, and God had removed Himself, but Joshua would not move. If Joshua was like any other person, then he had a list of prayer requests that he brought before the Lord, but his yearning was for something greater. It was Presence that he craved!

If you listen, truly listen to your prayers and the prayers of others, you will discover that our desperate desire is for Him to alleviate some form of suffering in our lives. We pray, and

- CHAPTER 1: YEARNING -

we pray again, over and over, asking for this thing or that other thing, but there is little mention of how we crave Him. I have noticed, and I'll bet you have, too, that people truly desperate for His touch for one debilitating disadvantage find that He often does more than expected. He not only meets their desperate need but becomes more personal, more known, more valued, and more trusted! For people with a reckless faith in the "dangerous God," there is a dawn that they did not ask for or expect. All they wanted was a simple answer to a specific prayer, but so much more was added to their life. They are not only healed, but now they know Him, really know Him! It's no longer knowledge about Him but a first-hand, face-to-face knowledge of who He is.

I'm pretty sure that is what you want, isn't it? I know that there are prayers I want to have answered, *but*...oh, how I crave His intimate presence. I long to know more and more of Him, to gaze upon the beauty of the Lord, and to dwell in His house forever. I want to be willing to risk like I did when I was young, when I had so little to lose! I not only want His intervention in my need, but I want to be able to pray: "I want more of You. Fill me with Your presence. I simply want more of You, no matter what You ask."

If you pray this prayer regularly, you will discover just how dangerously beautiful and intimate He can become. Pray this prayer, and you will move from the sidelines of faith into the game that is fraught with risk, but oh, so worth those risks because you will find Him!

What could happen in and through you, if found your first love again, you know, that one that is just a bit reckless in its pursuit of Him? Maybe it is time to ramp up your yearning for Him over the solution to your problem. Perhaps having Him would be more valuable than having the answer to that prayer you have been praying for so long. So, I invite you to keep reading so that you find what our heart truly desires…Him!

CHAPTER 2:
LABEL

> "Superficiality is the curse of our age. The doctrine of instant satisfaction is a primary spiritual problem. The desperate need today is not for a greater number of intelligent people, or gifted people, but for deep people."[7]
>
> —Richard Foster

A DISSATISFIED PEOPLE

Listen! Open your ears and open your eyes; we are essentially a dissatisfied people. Listen! You will hear it: the cry for change. Take note of almost any conversation today, and you will observe a common thread in most of them; it is the need for things to be different from what they currently are. There is a common longing for something different, but we are just not sure exactly what it is. Oh, everyone seems to have a strong opinion, but those opinions change with the ever-changing political and societal shifts. Change the political/societal season, and then you will notice a shift in opinions. It seems to me that everyone wants what they want, to the exclusion of all others. The theme of our age could easily be stated this way: agree with me about all things, then we will be friends; disagree with me on the smallest point, then we will forever be enemies. It's no wonder we crave something else. This is not how humanity was designed to live or interact!

There is one problem with all this enmity. It is that we are convinced that the problem exists outside of us. We believe that there is a great problem with the rest of humanity, but not within ourselves. If everyone else would just change, then we would have harmony and everlasting peace.

Have you noticed how this line of thinking is exactly like that found in the opening pages of human history? Adam said, "It was that woman you gave me." Eve said, "If there is anyone to blame, it is the serpent, not me." The serpent said, "It's God who is hiding truth from you." Even Cain passed off his murderous heart as existing outside himself, and humanity has been blaming everyone else since then.

I can't help but wonder if the change we crave is our inner voice calling for our transformation. Could it be that all our dissatisfaction with the world is an inner yearning in our spiritual core? Is it possible that the Spirit of God is whispering to you about your own needs? I know that from time to time I discover that my general dissatisfaction is really God's own Spirit calling me to examine my own heart. More often than not, I find that I need repentance, renewal, and reorientation. A common prayer for me is that prayer of David found in Psalm 51, *"Renew a right spirit within me."*[8]

A COMMON STORY

There are so many things that separate us from one another, but there is one common need for all of humanity, saints and sinners alike. It is the need to be conformed to the heart of God. The sinner longs for his spiritual peace and home of his own making, while the saint craves deepening relationship and intimacy found in an ever-increasing surrender.

If there is anything that truly binds us together, it is this: our need for our Creator and His love and mercy toward us. Because our transformation rests in His work in us, not in the renewal of others, He has made a way for even the most impotent to experience healing, restoration, and hope. Do you not know that we are the sum total of His creative mastery and our personal surrender?

What would happen to your world if you stopped looking outside yourself for the problems that cause you to be so disgruntled with others? How might others experience you if your daily prayer would include, *"Renew a right spirit with me?"*

If you and I are willing to pray that prayer, then your story and mine become stories that are evolving, growing, and transforming us into the image of His Son, Jesus Christ.

Just imagine that we were created with a purpose; we are His workmanship, but the blame game we play can take us out of the game.

SIDELINED

We all, each of us, are His unique and treasured creation. We are created in Christ Jesus, and we are prepared for a unique place in our world; you and I are not placed here randomly or haphazardly. This truth cannot be overstated! Each of us has a place and a purpose that has been ordained and called into existence by God Almighty Himself. That means that the life you now lead that can feel so small and powerless, in truth, is so much more. The scriptures are full of this truth from the first page to the last, but if we are honest, it is easy to forget this as we struggle under the weight of this life. Too often, we can feel pretty ordinary and small, and we too easily listen to the voice in our heads that reminds us just how weak we have been and how deep the pit created by our failures is. We still love the Lord and trust him for our salvation, but from time to time, we think about other Christians who seem to be so "put together." How can they be so blessed and able to navigate life with so much ease? Let me remind you that comparison isolates and is destructive! Ephesians 2:10 does not say that we are all mass-produced. It says, rather, that we are His unique workmanship. Like all living beings that, on the surface, appear to be exact copies, each of us is as unique as a leaf that is slightly different from all others on the same tree. They may look like exact copies, but they are not. God's creative workmanship never makes an exact copy of anything, you included. In fact, I'm so convinced of God's desire for uniqueness and intimate connection with his creation that I often imagine the Father saying to the Son and the Holy Spirit: "That blade of grass is stunning! Let's make another!" His joy overflows as He speaks each planet, each person, and each blade of grass into existence. He did not start the creation engine and then step back to watch how it all worked out. No! He remains intimately involved at every level of life.

Some Theologians will tell you that God's words and his actions are identical. In the flesh, we are so limited that we must first state our desires or intentions, and then we set out to make plans to do the work needed to match our words. We work to complete what we said. Not so with God. His words and His actions are identical. Here are some examples that may help clarify this for you. God said, "Let there be light," so naturally there was light. He did not declare an idea about light and then set out to make light. No, he spoke, making light a new reality because His words and His actions are identical. When God changed Abram's name to Abraham (father of nations), at that moment, Abram could not remain childless. When God speaks, His actions are a certainty.

So, what does this have to do with you and me and our situation? If God was so intimately involved in Abram's name change, He is just as involved in our creation and our destiny. I see it this way: there was a night when God whispered my name to my parents. Through their passions and physical connection, I was destined to be conceived. It was not guaranteed that I would be born or that I would be without defect, but His whisper could not be denied, so I was knit together in my mother's womb, and then, miraculously, I was born. Psalm 139 says it best: God's involvement in our creation and our life is an intimate and ongoing affair. This Psalm reminds me that He is actively involved in my creation, and He is active in bringing me to His desired end if I acknowledge and cooperate with Him and His plans.

Have you thought of your life in this way? Is it possible that He is that intimately involved in your life? Imagine, for just a moment, that I'm right and that one night, God whispered your name to your parents, and since His words and actions are identical, that whisper led to your birth. How does that make you feel to know that the God of all creation is connected to your existence? Before you spin off into some dark place because your life has had more than its share of trauma, take a breath. Now, think of all the others in this world who have suffered like you, then ask yourself, was God involved in their life? Of course He was! You do not have to look very far in the opening chapters of scripture to have that truth spoken by God Himself. He said of Pharaoh, "It was for this purpose that you were born."[9] It's always wonderful to think of God being responsible for you when life has been good, but not so much fun when you spend so much time recovering from all the muck and mire that the world dumps on you. Either way, God is involved and wants to continue to shape in you His perfect will and plans.

But unfortunately, there is a catch! There is an enemy who would do all in his power to cause us to stall, fall, or just give up, thus becoming a Christian side-liner. By "Christian side-liner," I mean people who acknowledge Jesus Christ as their Savior and do their best to be good members of society but are powerless and passionless in their walk with God. They have often been crushed by life, so they have moved from the field of surrendering to God to the sidelines of personal comfort. They pray, but it is usually for a meal or two each day. They may pray for blessings at the beginning or end of each day, but to think of prayer as a way to know God intimately is foreign and a bit scary. The Christian sideliner may not cause problems at home or church, but there is also little contribution to enriching the lives of others, and there is little spiritual power or authority. They say the right things, dress the right way, and separate themselves from everything that they believe may take them out of God's good graces. But authentic zeal, passion, or hunger for God's will and "presence" do not describe these people. Instead, words like safe, kind, and faithful, along with other benign words, can easily describe the Christian sideliner. Did they start their walk with Jesus this way? No, of course not! When a lost soul is found, there is a rush of newness that cannot be contained. Passion and zeal run at high levels. Spiritual hunger is satisfied in long sessions with scripture and meditating on the Word of God. But somewhere along the way, some Christians get sidelined, no longer in the game. You and I have seen players who dress for the game but who wait at the sidelines. They are dressed for the game, and they are present, but they are not in the game. Instead, others carry the ball and feel the pain and victory of the game. All the while, the sideliners are safe and pain-free. I have dressed for the game but waited happily and safely on the sidelines. I'll bet you have too.

So, the question that pops into my mind is, "What happened to sideline us?" Did we just get tired and worn out? Did the newness of our life in Christ just become routine? Could it be that the fear of not knowing what God would do in us, or through us, is what causes us to pull back to a safer place? Whatever the reason, addiction, brokenness, rejection, illness, hurt, or loss, we all face how we will respond to our spiritual disenfranchisement. Personally, I think that what happened to us is far more sinister than we may have considered. If God is so actively involved in calling and shaping us, then the enemy is just as active in moving us to the sidelines. He wants every person who calls on the name of Jesus to dress for the game but to wait on the sidelines, convinced that they don't have a calling or a greater destiny.

You may have been sidelined by something that you have considered to be a very small thing, or it may be something that feels like the world is crushing your spirit. Addiction, sin, willfulness, stubbornness, or another spiritual deficit may be what has held you captive on the sidelines. Whatever it is, you wonder if there is any hope for finding and fulfilling your God-designed destiny. If you are asking that question, then you are in a very good place! That question means that you are positioned for God's intervention. Get ready, things are about to change for you!

Diversion is the enemy's most effective strategy against me. Diversion keeps my attention focused elsewhere instead of my active pursuit of God's heart. Degree by degree, inch by inch, I find myself drifting off course. If I drift far enough, the memory of my original zeal is lost, and I develop a type of spiritual amnesia. This spiritual loss of memory opens the door for the enemy to speak lies more often and with greater authority. So, I become more and more double-minded, making me less and less effective in apprehending my God-deigned destiny. I get sidelined by my own imperceptible drift. I find that the Word of God is not top-of-mind for me any longer, which opens my mind to the lies of the enemy, making me unable to play effectively.

I hate that this happens to me! It is Romans chapter seven unfolding before my very eyes. I know that I am made for more, for a greater destiny than what I have experienced. I'll bet the same can be said of you. You pray, but those prayers feel like they reach no higher than the ceiling in your home. Perhaps you feel stale, powerless, unable to feel God's presence, and unsure at times if he even listens…to you. You sense that you are made for more than you are experiencing in Christ Jesus, but you have listened to the enemy for so long that you are not sure that you qualify for a more fulfilling life in Christ. Others may qualify, but not you.

The Scriptures are full of people just like you and I. They once had zeal and passion that moved them toward the heart of God, and His blessings were evident. But somehow, as they were tested, the distance between passion and safety grew, then grew more. But, as God always does, He waits until the condition of the heart is just right, and then He shows up most unexpectedly and at the most unexpected time.

In the chapters that follow, we will examine the life of one man who was as disenfranchised as one can become. In fact, his name actually means "unfit."

How would you like a label like that to follow you through life? Each time someone called his name, they were reminding him just how he did not measure up to God's destiny. He heard over and over that he was unfit for anything that God might want to do in him or for him. His label, plus the lies of the enemy, sidelined him for most of his life. But one day, a day that started just like all other days, he had an encounter with the One, who is the source of hope and healing. His story takes very little space in Scripture, but his story will inspire you and fill you with hope for a destiny in Christ. If the man labeled "unfit" can find his way from the sidelines to his destiny, so can you.

Let's begin with the collision that was Jesus' last journey through Jericho.

"And they came to Jericho."[10]

CHAPTER 3: COLLISION

> Collision: When two bodies come in direct contact with each other, the energy and momentum of those bodies interacting undergo a change as a result of the collision.

COLLISION COURSE

Two trains on the same track, traveling in opposite directions, will meet head-on to the great horror and terror of all those aboard. No one wants to witness this kind of catastrophic collision! Yet, other collisions give us reason to rejoice, to celebrate, to have hope in a God who can take a wreck of a life, reshaping it into something breathtakingly beautiful. Such is the collision of Jesus with the man they called "unfit." That collision renewed the one and glorified the other while causing all the bystanders to marvel and rejoice!

And they came to Jericho...[11]

Oh, how I love that short sentence! Do you understand that His coming to that place forever transformed lives? There are so many possibilities packed into that short sentence! There is no mention of how long they stayed or if they were just passing through. How many people did He stop to help as He and the disciples were there? Did He ignore all the crowds that followed Him, or was He asked to stop often? The Apostle John helps clear up some of the questions when he wrote, *"Now there are also many other things that Jesus did. Were every one of them to be written, I suppose that the world itself could not contain the books that would be written."*[12] It is clear from the Gospels that Jesus spent His days caring for people no matter where he found Himself. Why, even from the cross, He engaged John and His own mother to provide the hope they each needed. Pain and agony did not stop His caring heart. They are what drive Him! When Yahweh engaged Moses on Sinai, He provided His own self-disclosure. He passed before Moses and proclaimed, *"The Lord, the Lord, a God merciful and gracious, slow to anger, and abounding in steadfast love and faithfulness, keeping steadfast love for thousands, forgiving iniquity and transgression and sin."*[13] Do you notice that God does not begin His self-disclosure with, "I am a Holy and angry God who loves to punish sin and those who sin?" No, He is rich in mercy and grace! He is patient and slow to anger! He is steadfast and loving. He remains faithful even to those who struggle with their faithfulness. He is forgiving, and yes, He is altogether Holy! He hates sin but loves and moves quickly toward the contrite heart. You could easily say that He puts Himself on a collision course with those who seek His face and His heart! While there are times that He seems to be stealthy, most of the time, He moves clearly for all to see, inviting anyone who needs to move toward Him. That, my friend, is the significance of that opening sentence: **And they came to Jericho...**[14] Just like the encounter at the well outside Sychar *(see John, chapter 4)*, Jesus had an appointment that day in Jericho. You could easily say that He was on a collision course with Bartimaeus. Two trains traveling in opposite directions on the same track. Bartimaeus demonstrates just how desperately he wants this collision, all while Jesus shows His mercy and grace once again.

I could easily describe my own story in the same way. I was traveling at breakneck speed on the wrong track without regard to what lay ahead. I liked the speed and the illusion of freedom. I just wanted to feel like I was in full control of my life without anyone looking over my shoulder. But there was a day, on that very wrong track, that I ran smack dab into Jesus! We had a collision on my track, not His. He puts Himself where the need is the greatest. He climbed onto my track, knowing that I would never find myself on His, and then He traveled in my direction with resolute determination to let mercy, grace, and loving-kindness be the fallout from our collision. I'll wager that your story is not all that different from mine. You met Jesus in the most unexpected way and place. The ensuing collision reshaped your life and is now defined by His mercy, grace, and loving-kindness.

Or…perhaps you have been doing all in your power to define your life on your terms. You have felt the tug of God's mercy and grace, but to this point, you have, with resolute determination, refused to have your life any other way. He will allow that, you know. He is a gentleman, not forcing Himself on anyone. I know the analogy of a collision seems like you may have little to no choice in your encounter with God, but that's simply not true. You see, the remarkable thing about God is that He knows when you are open to His intervention. He will not intrude. He will not force Himself on you. But, and this is a big but…the scriptures make it clear that while He is patient and willing to wait for you, there is a final day appointed to everyone, and you don't know when that day will come and go. I hope that, while you have time remaining, you finally get to the place of surrender to His heart, that you allow that divine collision that Bartimaeus craved. Yes, he had a craving to see again, but he got so much more than he

- CHAPTER 3: COLLISION -

expected when he met Jesus just outside Jericho. He asked for new eyes, but Jesus, as He always does, had so much more in mind for blind Bartimaeus. And I am certain that He has more in mind for you. Won't you just simply relax and breathe a simple prayer, asking Him to do for you what He did for the man known as "unfit." If Bartimaeus was known as "unfit" and Jesus more than met his need, He will do the same for you. Why not take a moment to pray right now?

DESTROYING BARRIERS

You need to know that Mr. Unfit was very naturally an outcast. He was separated from the crowd, unable to participate with the population at large, except, of course, when begging. He was thought of and treated as one who did not qualify for love, attention, or relationship. Remarkably, by the time we get to the end of his story, we see him invited into the most significant relationship of all. Jesus showed up in Jericho, and while He was on His way out of town, He showed us how He was the destroyer of barriers as He and Bartimaeus collided. The Apostle Paul wrote about it this way.

"... *making known to us the mystery of his will, according to his purpose, which he set forth in Christ as a plan for the fullness of time, to unite all things in him, things in heaven and things on earth."*[15]

If your world is anything like mine, then your heart craves a more peaceful existence. It seems that everywhere I look, everyone is pointing an accusing finger at everyone else! I would say we now live in a culture of entitlement and blame. "I'm entitled to what I want or what I believe, and you are to blame for why I don't have it," seems to be the attitude I run into daily. Sadly, this attitude is overtaking the church, which, as you know, is called to live above all this nonsense. Jesus said that we are to be known by our love, not our strong opinions. Did He not invite Judas into His inner circle? Did He not serve him by washing his feet, then by including him in that Last Supper just before that night's betrayal?

We long for a more harmonious world, and we know that only Jesus can make that a reality. We want all differences wiped away so that the world looks and feels more comfortable to us. We want the world to fit our assumptions and our likes, yet all around us, in front of our very eyes, He has provided a world so varied in terrain and plant life that it is astoundingly beautiful! Have you ever seen an animal or a sea creature that caused you to think, "What was God thinking when He made that one?"

It would appear that God is showing us that even in a world of vastly different flora and fauna, they can live together, work together, and contribute to the overall beauty of the world.

When harmony exists in a family, church, or community, it is a wonder to behold. Vastly different people living, working, and contributing together. I believe we need a reality check and need to be reminded that Jesus did not bring harmony by removing differences but by destroying barriers! The differences of race and gender are not eliminated but sanctified under His authority. We remain the gender and race to which we were born, but the barriers that kept us apart no longer need to exist, that is, unless we choose to re-erect them. Jesus did not bring harmony by removing differences but by destroying barriers; the barriers that once kept us at a distance from God have been destroyed. We remain sinful by nature but are adopted into The Family. We have been invited in but remain individuals who are vastly different from one another. Family and harmony are not dependent on sameness but on acceptance and love.

The point of all this is that Mr. Unfit was forced to live in the shadows. He was invisible to everyone, except when he was doing something embarrassing, like screaming at Jesus. The people who were charged by the very law they swore to uphold rewrote that law to fit their desired comfort level. I know that I am always more comfortable when I don't have to see suffering in person. That's the way it was in Jericho. If you were blind, then you became invisible out of convivence for everyone else; your needs or desires mattered little. They had erected barriers that separated people and kept the undesirables far from view. I wonder, does any of this ring true in your life? Are there people that you hold in disdain or relegate to an invisible state? I have always been surprised and disappointed by how easily we in the Church do these things. Is there someone whom you have labeled as "unfit"? Perhaps it's time for your own divine collision in this matter.

DIVINE COLLISIONS

Spoiler alert! In the next few chapters, we will see what a divine collision can do in the life of even the most rejected and unworthy seeker. We will observe what an unrestrained hunger for God can do for the one who is willing to risk everything to possess what cannot be gained through self-effort. We will see grace in action, and we will learn that we can live in that same plane of unrestrained hunger and delight.

Sometimes, I wonder about this moment in Jericho. Did

it just happen or was there more going on here than this short passage reveals? Once again, theologians have a word for it. Prevenient Grace is that grace of God that precedes our needs. Paul was referring to the "grace that goes before" when he wrote to the Ephesian church.

He said... *even as He chose us in Him before the foundation of the world, that we should be holy and blameless before Him. In love, He predestined us for adoption to Himself as sons through Jesus Christ, according to the purpose of His will...*

His plan from before time began. He was to offer the grace of adoption to all who would receive that grace. For some crazy reason, the God of the universe wants to be in a family relationship with us, and for that, I am astounded and grateful! But the questions still haunt me: why Jericho? Why **that** day? Why **that** road? I know that it would not be too difficult to provide a reasonable explanation for **that** road on **that** day, but I have been on the receiving end of His prevenient grace. I know firsthand how beyond explanation His timing can be. I've held in my hands His miraculous gifts, and I've seen with my own eyes works of grace and mercy that cannot be explained any other way. So, I'm sure that Jesus showed up on the road on that day because there was one who was unfit to be part of anyone's family, let alone God's family! Prevenient grace once again met one more need because nothing makes God's heart sing more than to find one rejected and isolated person who is willing to abandon hopelessness to find everlasting hope in Jesus.

I hope you know that all divine collisions are not always just happenstance. You may not have planned your collision, but it came to you nonetheless. So, I would submit that Jesus had a divine collision ahead of Him, and Bartimaeus had a choice waiting for him. Would he remain invisible, blending into the dusty background of the road outside Jericho, or would he become visible for all to see? Bartimaeus had a choice to make.

CHOICES

It appears to me that the most consistently spiritual thing we do daily is choose. If you take a moment to review your life, you will notice that each good or bad move you have made has been preceded by a choice. That day you said "yes" to Jesus was a day that you could have said "no" as well. Our days are full of choices, and it is primarily in this arena that our life's strength and direction are set. Choose righteousness, and you are choosing life, according to *Deuteronomy 30:11–20*. Choosing your own path brings death, according to this passage as well.

- CHAPTER 3: COLLISION -

Adam and Eve each made a choice, and so has every person who has drawn a breath since that devastating day. Choices can make or break us, so please use your choices to find life rather than death. Choose service over being served. Choose to follow Jesus closely, even when the road leads to an unexpected cross.

In the coming chapters, we will notice that a choice to move from invisibility to visibility was answered because "Mr. Unfit" was willing to risk everything to have his needs met. I'm pretty sure that you have your own unmet need, something in your life that needs a divine collision. The question is, how far are you willing to trust that divine collision? Don't be fooled! Collisions, all collisions, change the people involved; there is a price to be paid. For Bartimaeus, it was throwing off all restraint while asking for one thing: new eyes. As we progress through this short passage of scripture, we will discover that Bartimaeus was frantic for a solution to his immediate need. He was willing to put everything on the line to get a chance to have just one moment with Jesus. The problem was that he would face resistance! Would he listen to the crowd telling him to move back into the shadows, or would he follow his own heart so that he might have one everlasting divine collision?

CHAPTER 4:
QUESTIONS AND DECISIONS

> "We do not see our signs; there is no longer any prophet, and there is none among us who knows how long. How long, O God, is the foe to scoff? Is the enemy to revile your name forever."[16]

WHERE IS YOUR GOD?

Why is there suffering if God is so good? This is one of the most difficult questions all people encounter as they wrestle with the meaning of life. It is often spoken in mocking tones by those who reject God and faith in Him. It is whispered by people of faith because no one wants to appear to lack real faith. But it is a question that, at some point, makes it to the lips of all people who are aware of the wide world around them.

You may be one of those who know, first hand, the weight of suffering. Either you or someone close to you has experienced the worst that life can serve up. Chances are that you have asked the "Why suffering?" question often because your life is so completely occupied by suffering's presence. Thus, you may have given up on what faith in God can do because your prayers have not been answered as you expected.

CHAPTER 4: QUESTIONS AND DECISIONS

You may be one of the lucky ones whose life is pretty good. You have had setbacks and heartbreak, but real suffering has not found its way into your home. If this is your life, I'll bet that you have asked the suffering question about children and other people you know who have suffered greatly.

The question of suffering is just one of those theological conundrums that seem to go on and on without any satisfactory answer. We want God's movement to match our assumptions, and we want Him to move unilaterally to alleviate all suffering. We want heaven to comply with our perceptions of how life should work, and we tend to question God's motives when suffering is laid before our eyes. What's worse is those who reject a life surrendered to God begin to loudly question His existence and His goodness. They demand answers that no one can seem to give. It appears to me that a lack of true faith can never be satisfied because it's easier to mock than believe.

We all know that God is able to do anything, especially when it comes to ending suffering and debilitating illness, but His lack of intervention just seems senseless and appears to contribute to the chaotic lives of those who truly suffer. So, your question morphs just a bit because you know He is able, but for some reason, your prayers seem to skip across heaven like a stone across a pond. Your new prayer becomes, "Where are You, God? Why are You willing to meet other needs while You ignore mine?"

I wonder if this was the question that blind Bartimaeus was asking. We are not told how long he suffered, but we know that his suffering was compounded by his loss of the sight that he once had. When asked by Jesus what he, Bartimaeus, would like, his answer was to *"see again."*[17] Bartimaeus knew sight, and he knew blindness. He knew goodness, and he very likely knew bitterness. To lose one's hearing is a disaster. To lose the ability to communicate is more than frustrating; it is hellish. But to lose sight is to be locked in an inescapable prison that shrinks your world to the length of your reach. Bitterness could follow any of these losses. Did they find their way into Bartimaeus? It's possible because he had a reputation. He was, according to one theologian, "the son of filth."[18] When you lose your sight and are reminded how people label you each time they speak your name, bitterness will generally overshadow all hope. He could remain as he had been, hidden in the shadows, holding on to all the reasons his life was worthless, or he could jettison all the questions and labels and decide to pursue another course of action. Could there be some glimmer of hope in that blind, unfit son of filth?

CHAPTER 4: QUESTIONS AND DECISIONS

THE EXCHANGE

Bartimaeus had a decision to make! Would he continue to live in the shadows, in what was a life of darkness, or would he push the boundaries of cultural norms by becoming the most visible person in that crowd? Would the man called the "unfit son of filth" choose to throw off restraint, or would he remain on the very familiar and somewhat comfortable sidelines? Bartimaeus had a choice set before him. Either new eyes or the familiar status quo of darkness and begging. As with all important decisions, there is an exchange that must take place. He would have to say "no" to one thing so that he could say "yes" to something else. That's how important choices are made. You exchange one thing for another. Nothing is free, and these exchanges are not easy. I'll bet you have noticed that there are people who want a limitation of theirs to go away, but…it is familiar, and they have grown somewhat comfortable with it, so the exchange comes very slowly, if at all. I've watched this in my own life. I know that I need to jettison some debilitating part of my inner life, yet it has been there all my life, and saying no to that thing will cause me to exchange a very familiar part of who I am for some new and wholly unfamiliar thing. How can I be sure that it would work for me? So far, my life is manageable, and I like manageable! The truth is, just like Bartimaeus, there is a choice set before us. Will we throw off restraint to have all that Jesus has for us, or will we remain hidden in the familiar but uncomfortable shadows?

As I have already stated, the most spiritual activity that you engage in daily is the activity of choosing. Prayer is important, and so is time in scripture. Private and corporate worship are vital to your spiritual life, but choices will set the trajectory of your life. It is because of your choices that you will soar or sink. Joshua said it this way: *"...choose this day whom you will serve, whether the gods your fathers served in the region beyond the River, or the gods of the Amorites in whose land you dwell. But as for me and my house, we will serve the LORD."*[19]

Now, I know that this verse is referring to one of those *big* choices we make, the choice of whom we will worship and to whom we pledge our loyalty, but at the base of this particular choice is just how much of our life will be touched by this choice. You do know, I hope, that your life will travel in the direction of your most consistent choices. We like to think that it is large, significant moments that set the direction of our lives, so we wait and watch for big moments and weighty decisions while paying very little attention to the mundane moments, the insignificant decisions. But life is made up of millions of moments, and choices made within all those moments set the ultimate arc of your life. So, no choice is without some spiritual weight. If your life in Christ is meant to manifest His presence and glory, then your moments and your choices do matter a great deal. But, too often, the choices we make are influenced more by the label we wear than who we are in Christ. He says that He fully redeemed us, but we have a vivid memory of our every shortfall, so we live well below that redemption. He makes it clear, in scripture, that we are each designed to make Him known through our unique place in this world, yet we hold back. We are undeniably called to serve others who are in need, but our own needs limit how willing we are to respond to God's call. The sidelines of personal comfort are a real temptation for every Christ follower. But "Mr. Unfit" shows us a way out. He demonstrates, for all to see, what can happen when you choose Jesus, really choose Him, over the familiar that has grown vaguely comfortable.

WHAT WOULD YOU DO?

Average is always a safe choice, and it's the most dangerous choice you can make.[20] While the trajectory of a life is set in all the little moments and choices, some choices are more consequential than others, and now and then, there is a life-altering moment that has the potential to unlock all our hopes and dreams. This is that moment for Bartimaeus!

And when he heard that it was Jesus of Nazareth, he began to cry out and say, "Jesus, Son of David, have mercy on me!" And many rebuked him, telling him to be silent. But he cried out all the more, "Son of David, have mercy on me!"[21]

Jesus' reputation had preceded Him. Whispers and some open conversations about the wandering prophet who heals people have reached Jericho. Naturally, there were some questions about this prophet, and these questions always led to debates about His political station. So far, the prophecies about the coming Messiah were manifesting themselves in Jesus. Could He be the One? Could He be trusted to deliver the nation from bondage just as He had delivered some people from the bondage of illness and deformity? It is interesting to note that twice Bartimaeus refers to Jesus by His Messianic title, which refers to Him as the conquering hero that Israel awaited—"Son of David." This is the title reserved for those who sit on the throne of Israel. "Son of David" is a political and deliverer title. That means that while Bartimaeus had heard about the healings, he did not have a full understanding of who Jesus is. Bartimaeus indeed wanted healing just like others had received, but he had a small earth-bound vision of Jesus. Thankfully, that misconception and limited view by Bartimaeus did not limit Jesus. No, He was about to prove that so much more awaited Bartimaeus than was expected. But to get to that moment, Bartimaeus had to respond to an invitation; he had a decision to make, and he needed to follow through on that decision.

Keep in mind that he wore a label that had held him in the shadows of that dusty road. He lived in obscurity and depended on the kindness of others for his very existence. Everything that he had known that was a blessing had been forcibly taken from him through the blindness that kept him prisoner. Now ask yourself, "What would I do if I were Bartimaeus?" Your answer and mine would be to do just what Bartimaeus had done. Make some noise, a lot of noise! But I would remind you that we know the end of the story, but he did not! Too often, we are quick to answer questions like this, in this way, when it has not been the actual pattern of our life. To throw off restraint while pushing against cultural norms takes courage. And all too often, we choose to do the safe thing. What Bartimaeus did was nothing short of courageous. He threw off personal and cultural restraints as he called out for Jesus over and over. The crowd around him did their best to remind him of his place. They did their best to silence him because, as you know, he was unfit!

I can't help but wonder about your situation and your secret but defining label. I wonder if you have an earth-bound understanding of Jesus. Have you shrunk back as others have worked to silence your cry for help? Is this your moment? Could this book be your Jericho Road? Is it possible that Jesus is passing by, and is this your chance to have Him address you and your needs? Will you throw off all your past restraints to call on the One who is more than able to meet your needs? Will you move toward Him without fear but with expectation? Bartimaeus did that! Expectation filled him and gave him the courage to throw off all restraint as he moved toward Jesus the Healer.

CHAPTER 5: BREAKTHROUGH

> Pray...Yield...Believe...Obey and see what God will do for you over the next few weeks.

DESPERATE

Few things in life are more difficult to bear than suffering that seems meaningless or unwarranted. But this is often the platform for real breakthroughs. Meaningless suffering breeds desperation, and desperation can open the door to real, life-altering action. The problem with suffering and desperation being linked together is that the action that the desperation causes will take one of two forms: action guided by resentment/bitterness or action steered by hope-filled surrender. Remarkably, Bartimaeus' desperation took that second, hope-filled route.

All too often people who have suffered, as he had, will demand that God give an accounting of His actions for their suffering. They demand answers to their own why questions. Why me? Why now? And why this kind of unjust suffering? Most people tend to look for cause-and-effect answers to all the uncomfortable things they endure. We want to affix the blame.

We want to know who to hold accountable for all this tragedy and pain. Was it a bug that I picked up somewhere, was it that guy who cut me off in traffic, was it some sin in my life, or does God just hate me? On and on, we go looking for a place to park our blame. A quick question. Does this describe you in some way? If it does, would you be surprised if I told you that you are in a very good place? You see, as I have grown to know the Sovereign God, who knows you perfectly, I have discovered that He is working deeply in you to create in you a heart that is desperate for Him. He is waiting for you to get desperate for Him rather than for answers to your demanding questions. Your uncomfortable desperation can move you toward Him without reservation if you do what Bartimaeus did. There can be no holding back on your part. He is ready to move into your desperate and unfair situation so that you experience more than the reduction of your pain. This kind of desperation moves you toward God's heart, and it is there, connected to God's heart, that real transformation takes place.

That is what is about to happen to Bartimaeus. He will get new eyes and, oh, so much more! Watch in awe and wonder as Bartimaeus throws off all restraint, and while you are watching him, think about your own desperate need. The collision that will take place on that Jericho Road will change him physically

- CHAPTER 5: BREAKTHROUGH -

and spiritually. Please don't look away; you need to see what happens as a result of this beautiful collision between a blind, unfit beggar and the Lord of the universe.

BREAKTHROUGH

"And Jesus stopped and said, 'Call him.' And they called the blind man, saying to him, 'Take heart. Get up; he is calling you.' And throwing off his cloak, he sprang up and came to Jesus."[22]

Is it possible that blind Bartimaeus felt that his suffering was undeserved, or did he blame himself and his circumstances? After all, his name was "unfit." I wonder how long he sat next to that road. I ask myself if he resented his life or if he hated God, even just a little bit. The sight that he once had and his ability to navigate life are now gone, and all his losses only served to lock him into a dusty corner while he begged for help. Whatever his mental and spiritual state, it is clear that desperation was now the beat of his heart. He wanted nothing more than the resolution of his need. He had heard the crowd as they were passing by, and they made it clear that Jesus was there. But the crowd also made it very clear that while Jesus was here: "He is not here for the likes of you, so be quiet, know your place. It's over there in the dust where no one needs to notice you."

Every one of us can feel that way at some point in our life, relegated to the outskirts of all that matters to us, while we feel isolated from hope and help. There are so many things that can cause us to take up residence on our own Jericho Road. The death of a loved one, the loss of a relationship that we trusted, our health decline, financial loss, the loss of a job, an addiction of any kind, or any one of a thousand other things. Suffering comes in so many forms, but it always causes us to experience some inward isolation and questioning. But here is just a bit of good news. You can escape just like Bartimaeus did. How he did it is so simple that you may be tempted to dismiss the idea as too simplistic. You might just think that a renewed life has to be more complicated than this.

I've already alluded to the two key components that Bartimaeus shows us: *desperation* and the *willingness* to throw off restraint. Allow me to walk you through these two ideas and how they brought him face-to-face with Jesus.

It is not clear in scripture, but somewhere and at some time on that dusty road, Bartimaeus became so frustrated with the way things were in his life that he decided that he must do some things differently. Specifically, he would not squander any opportunity if Jesus ever came his way. You know, don't you, that missed opportunities are quite common in our spiritual life. Life can become comfortable and familiar, even when we carry some scar or spiritual impediment. Change is hard and often fearsome, so opportunities to address our real needs appear, then disappear as we hesitate. A door of opportunity is thrown open and then slowly closes as we debate within ourselves, counting the cost of change. This does not mean that the door won't reopen, but it does mean with each hesitation, it becomes easier to hesitate again, to just accept things the way they are. So, each choice to hold on to our uncomfortable but very familiar life increases the distance between open doors. Eventually, we just accept things the way they are. Not so with Bartimaeus! It is evident that he had made up his mind that he would let nothing stand between his need and Jesus, so he became desperate, and that desperation showed up in his voice. He cried out; then he cried out some more! Everything and everyone did their best to quiet that desperately loud voice. It was disruptive, it was out of place, and it kept people from experiencing Jesus while He walked through Jericho. Bartimaeus got pushback from the crowd, yet he cried out all the more! And, if his mind worked in any way like mine, then he also received some internal pushback. His mind screamed, *"Quiet, you don't deserve real help!"*

But somehow, Bartimaeus forced himself past all the other voices insisting on his silence. He responded to the open door and invitation standing before him.

Have you ever watched someone throw off all restraint so that they can experience what they fully desire? It is an amazing thing to witness. There is no thought about what other people may think or what hazards lie ahead; they only want that thing that has always been just out of reach. So, they cast off all fear and inhibition that has held them back so that they can rush headlong toward their greatest desire.

If you have been around children or have your own, or are the proud grandparent of a little one who does not know caution, then you have seen with your own eyes what pure, unfettered fearlessness can accomplish.

In my own life, I have one very vivid memory of this kind of behavior. Full disclosure here! The reason this comes to mind so easily is because I was the object of desire. I can still see our youngest granddaughter in the living room of her home. Her grandmother and I had just arrived, and our daughter had just opened the door for us. From across the room, our eyes locked. Then, that toddler ran toward me with a gleeful scream. On the way, she pushed aside her older sister, her mother, and her grandmother as she rocketed toward me! She leaped into my arms with a squeal of delight while clinging to my neck. What a memory! While I'm being honest here, I have seen her do the very same thing with her other grandfather. Apparently, our youngest loves her grandpas. The point is that this memory always brings a smile to my face and quickens my heart rate just a bit. Why? Because being someone's greatest desire establishes our worth and connects the two individuals with a bond few people know.

Every time I think of our granddaughter living an unrestrained life, I think of Jesus and Bartimaeus.

Bartimaeus became a bit unhinged as Jesus approached. So much so that some translations of the Bible make it clear that the crowd was embarrassed by his inappropriate behavior, so they tried to shut him up. The harder they tried to redirect Bartimaeus, the louder and more determined he became. The commotion became so evident that it could not be ignored, so Jesus pushed the pause button. Then he said to the crowd, "Tell him I'm here, and he can come to me." Now, this is another one of those Bible passages that has just bothered me. Bartimaeus is blind; Jesus is not. But He wants that blind guy to find his way to Him through that thick crowd. It just doesn't sit well with me. I want Jesus to validate Bartimaeus by going to him. I want Jesus, in grace, to take the first step and make the move toward the need that is before him. But he doesn't. He calls, and Bartimaeus throws off all restraint. Jesus knows that faith, real faith, is needed to cross that threshold of opportunity. Look at Mark 10:50: *"And throwing off his cloak, he sprang up and came to Jesus."* Notice how packed that sentence is with *pathos*! The line just drips with emotion and passion. Bartimaeus throws off his cloak, that outer garment that was meant to be a full protection from the elements. It was heavy, and it was meant to cover him from head to foot. If there was anything other than his blind eyes that would slow his journey to Jesus, it would be that cloak. So, he throws it off. Then he does a marvelous and unexpected thing. He springs! He did not stand. He did not get up. He sprang up! Now, please hold on here because I'm going to let the *pathos* and action words in that sentence permit me to finish the scene with my imagination. In my mind, since he threw off restraint and then sprang up, then he must have run, too. This is a man who, in this hour, knew no inhibition! The one desire of his heart was near, and nothing was going to hold him back. Not a cloak, not a crowd, and certainly not blind eyes, nor unsteady feet that could not move fast enough. I can picture this man so desperate for Jesus and new eyes that he leaned forward with arms outstretched as he moved as fast as his feet would carry him. Can you imagine the scene? He jumps up and begins to move, so the crowd parts, giving him a clear path to his Healer and Savior.

I want to live my life with Jesus like this man. I want to be like a blind man running, unconcerned by anything that may be in my path so that I can have the desire of my heart, Jesus! I want my private and public worship to be like this: unrestrained. I want my prayer life to be this uninhibited. I want to know Him. I want to lock eyes from across the room, then run into his arms, clinging to him. Do you know why? Because He has called my name, He has invited me, and my healing awaits.

The question is, does this idea resonate with you, or is it intimidating? If there is part of you that hesitates because this kind of abandoned worship and pursuit of God would cost you too much, then I have some hard news for you. God always works to move us forward into a deeper, more faith-filled life. He desires that we have a greater capacity for faith and love. Since you have now witnessed what it is like to live like a blind man running, He will continually call you back to this idea. He will not let the idea rest until you become desperate, throwing off all that hinders you. This is the kind of life He desires for all who are His. I think that is what makes Bartimaeus so compelling. His hunger and willingness to cast aside all that would hinder him is a damning witness against our desire for control. I will remind you that we too often choose lack of spiritual fervor over even the slightest excess. My question for you is this: Is that really the way you want to live in a relationship with Him, saying, "You can come this far, but no farther?" I've done that; it is not a good place to be. Limiting God's access will always be honored by Him, but it will always result in small living and long spiritual detours.

My invitation to you is to jump and run! Permit Him full access by casting aside all that you have tried to control. Abandon your desire to have your spiritual life on your terms. Cast off that cloak, spring to your feet, and run into His perfect mercy. Who knows how He may meet your needs? Have you forgotten what the scriptures say: "He knows we are but dust, but loves us supremely"?[23] He formed us and knows our every thought but "hems us in, behind, and before."[24] He puts His mighty hand on us, such knowledge is too high to attain![25] That protective cloak of self-abasement that you wear needs to be thrown off. Stop delaying, stop making excuses. He knows you completely, yet He invites you to: "Come to Me." This could be your moment of breakthrough.

CHAPTER 6:
RECOVERY

"And Jesus said to him, 'What do you want me to do for you?' And the blind man said to him, 'Rabbi, let me recover my sight.'"[26]

THIEVES

From the opening pages of scripture through much of the book of Revelation, we are confronted with the story and results of Paradise Lost. What God designed and ordained has been, for a brief time, taken; humanity has been robbed! We have lost peace, safety, relational harmony, and oh, so much more. Our lives and our world have been splintered by all that was stolen, but for the sake of love, we need to remind each other that this theft is a temporary condition because…the thieving continues until He finally returns.

The primary request on the lips of Bartimaeus was to regain what he had lost; he had been robbed! Whether it was the intense light of the Middle Eastern sun, some disease, or an accident matters little. What is central issue for this unfit, blind beggar was that he no longer had what was once a normal part of his life.

"Let me recover my sight," was his simple but singular request. Bartimaeus knew what was missing because it was physical. Every moment of every day, he was limited by his own body, but I'll wager that there were more than eyes that needed a divine touch. That original robbery in the Garden has left its mark on every person who has ever drawn a breath. We are broken, and because every other person we meet is also broken, we begin to treat brokenness as routine and somewhat acceptable. Have you noticed how we so easily make excuses for our fractured souls but require perfection from others? Which, if you think about it, clearly shows the depth of our self-centered and shattered lives.

The point is this: you, too, have lost something precious. It may be physical, but most likely, some part of your soul has been taken. A thief has broken in to take a part of you that you desire to regain. So, our common story does its best to self-solve problems. We turn to our own strengths or to self-help courses, books on self-esteem, motivational conferences, and the list goes on. Honestly, there is nothing inherently wrong with any of these things; they do help. I have used every one of the ideas in this list to help lift my life and effectiveness, but to not turn to Jesus, first and primarily, is to feed the dysfunction that already lives within us. He is our Source. He is the Savior and Sustainer. He is our Healer and Hope. Without Jesus at the center of our lives, we drift off into the dark and dangerous waters of self-absorption. We become our source as we look within ourselves for answers rather than seeking the author of life. So, the thieving continues. We find our souls plundered by so many things. Most we can name without much thought. Things like rebellion, addiction, pornography, secret sin, hate, the overt practice of making others less than yourself, and so much, much more. But other fissures of the soul are equally as damaging and are less noticeable to us. That is unless you do a thorough self-assessment. Here are a few ideas that may just speak to you.

THROTTLED TRUST

Any time we limit God's access to our whole life, we set ourselves up for disaster. This is a choice for self over our Creator and Savoir and is most often found in those who are most concerned about how others perceive them. The larger your trust in how others see you, the more you will likely dictate to God how your life should flow. In addition to longing to have a good public image, a throttled-down trust in God will also control how you manage your personal resources. Money, status, possessions, and other things will replace God as the one you trust most. Here is a good test. How are you participating in the kingdom of God with your money? The reason so many pastors keep bringing this up is that they know that money is the one tangible thing that is directly tied to the spiritual realm. It is tied to the spiritual realm in this way: where you direct your money most often is the thing you most trust. This is not to say that you must give everything, but scripture is pretty clear about partnering with God with your possessions. How are you doing with your financial trust?

You may have been hurt in some way by the church, or by people that you trusted, or even by God Himself, that you quietly have whispered, "That will never happen again!" I actually had a season in my life when the hurt was so deep that I said, "God, I love You, but never ask me to do anything like that again. You can have most of me, but I reserve this part of me for myself; You can come into my life only so far, but no farther." This one statement only increased the hurt and distance between me and God because my trust was throttled. The journey back has been long and sometimes difficult, but so worth it. There is a freshness and increased trust because He and I have gotten past all the hurt and confusion.

Keep in mind that trust and desire are tethered. Jesus said that your heart will always travel in the direction of your strongest desire.[27] The question you need to consider is, where do your desires lie? Is He the true desire of your heart, or is His blessing of more value to you?

UNWORTHINESS

Any Throttled Trust will eventually lead to an increased distance between you and God, which in turn opens you to other voices, voices that care nothing for your welfare, only your limitation. The reason that your limitations are targeted by the enemy is that he knows what you are capable of when you fully and humbly submit to God. You only need to read the Gospels and the book of Acts to get a realistic picture of what is possible. Power and victory are yours, just as they were for the Disciples. The problem is that we have so limited our trust and desire for God that other voices bombard us with a sense of unworthiness. Voices, like those who spoke to Bartimaeus, often speak to us as well. They say, "Stay where you are, you don't qualify, you are not worthy." Nothing could be further from the truth! You know the story of the Prodigal Son, but have you made a personal application? Have you realized that you are the child of the Most

High God? Do you know that He is merciful and gracious? *(See God's description of Himself in Exodus 34:6.)* Have you let His mercy and grace have unfettered access to your soul? Again, I ask, have you traded your desire for Him for something less than Him? How long are you going to live in that "unworthy" zip code? Perhaps it is time to throw off all that unworthiness so that you can live your life like a blind man running!

EMPTINESS

Listening to voices that declare you unworthy will always create a void in your soul that you will desire to fill. I know you noticed how you try to fill your life with things meant to quiet the agitation in your spirit. Emptiness whispers to you in the quiet hours. It disturbs your soul and fills your mind with questions and some level of dread. Is it any wonder that you find sleep difficult or that you turn to food, alcohol, toxic relationships, or other things? We want to feel some significance, so we turn to anything that makes us feel better. We all know the scientific principle that nature abhors a vacuum. The same principle exists in the spiritual realm as well. Your soul will gravitate toward anything that can fill that empty space in your heart. You know this, but still, you have been reluctant to face it because you know the emptiness too well, it is familiar, and familiar can feel somewhat comfortable. Besides, that emptiness in you is not all that large, and you think that you can manage it all on your own.

Think for a moment about the emptiness that Bartimaeus must have felt because the world declared him to be unworthy. He was isolated and rejected. We do not know the details of his personal life aside from his blindness, but we do know that he was called "son of filth" and "unfit," so somewhere in him was an empty place that needed Jesus' divine touch. Bartimaeus let his hunger for vision propel him into the very presence of his Healer and Savior. As I have already stated, he got new eyes, but since he attached himself to Jesus by following Him after he was healed, we know that he had another part of his spirit repaired. That is the way Jesus works! He always gives more than asked. He adds on!

There is hope for you, too. You may crave something altogether different, but His divine touch will fill that emptiness that haunts you. Take hope, my friend. He can meet your needs while filling that void that haunts you. So once again, I must ask, "What is your deepest desire?" Will you remain mired in your known emptiness, or will you throw off that cloak that hinders you? Will you be willing to jump up, then run head-long into the arms of the One who can fill all that emptiness? Come on, there is no one telling you to stay in the shadows. No one but the enemy is calling you unworthy, so do what you must to find yourself in Jesus' presence. He is near, waiting. Why are you waiting to run to Him?

ANGER/BITTERNESS

I already know that you have dismissed these two because they can't possibly pertain to you and your life. The problem with that thought process is that these two destroyers are very subtle, disguising themselves as something more noble. Just like camouflage clothing that hides the one wearing them, bitterness and anger can disguise themselves so that they are masquerading and hidden, appearing to be something else altogether. Have you noticed that your anger or bitterness always exists because of what someone else has done, never because of what is actually going on in your own heart? Anger and bitterness will always have you blame someone else for your problems while ignoring all that is going on in your soul. Anger and bitterness are so easily justified, making you feel more righteous than the one who caused the anger. You are the victim; they are the perpetrator! You are innocent, while others or your circumstances are the reason you feel so angry. Sound a bit more familiar now? I'm not trying to pry, but I am praying that you throw off all that holds you captive. You can find freedom from the endless cycles of hurt and self-justification. You can find your healing in the arms of your ally, Jesus, if you will just give up your prerogative to be right.

CYNICISM/CONTROL

Like bitterness and anger, cynicism, along with its twin, the need for control, disguises itself as something altogether different. They do not want to be accurately identified because these two give the one who wears them the illusion of a feeling of superiority. You know as well as I that being in control feels really good! The problem is that too often, we use these as tools to elevate our station in life while reducing others. There was a time in my life when these two helped me feel so much better about myself but left a very bitter taste in my mouth. How can we so easily disregard and minimize others? The problem with living like this is that the law of reciprocity (you may know it as karma) will kick in sometime in the future. Eventually, I found myself on the receiving end of cynicism and control. I began to experience first-hand how hurtful I had been to others.

I deeply regret that season and sometimes wish I could relive those moments so that I could be more gracious.

I have noticed that each of these fractures of the soul drains life from those who live with them. No wonder Bartimaeus was so desperate to make himself visible to Jesus. He had been living with his inner life draining away, feeling more of the weight of unworthiness daily. And, if he was anything like you and me, then bitterness and anger had crept in to steal his peace. But at some point, he decided to do what was necessary to meet the itinerant preacher-healer that he heard so much about. His desire for healing kicked in, and it was his desire that moved him from his unworthy, invisible status to one whose needs were met from the inside out!

DESIRE

The Apostle Paul asked the right question in his letter to the Romans: *"Who will deliver me from this body of death?"*[28] He had lived a life that sought to control others while he gave full permission to his anger and bitterness. He wanted to live a righteous life, but he desired to control. He found life to be empty and confusing:

> So I find it to be a law that when I want to do right, evil lies close at hand. For I delight in the law of God, in my inner being, but I see in my members another law waging war against the law of my mind and making me captive to the law of sin that dwells in my members. Wretched man that I am! Who will deliver me from this body of death?[29]

Paul's desire was to be freed from all that held him captive, and he was, as he submitted his life to the Lordship of Jesus.

As I have already stated, your life will always travel in the direction of your greatest desire. So, my question remains: What is it that you truly desire? What are you willing to give up to find it?

I can't help but wonder if the desire of that blind, unfit beggar had some effect on those who watched this miraculous moment unfold. Honestly, it affects me! Compared to all my unrestrained moments, this one seems other-worldly. It is so outside of what is normal for me and most people I know; it is hard for me to grasp this kind of desperation. Don't get me wrong; my heart swells with a deeper desire to run to Jesus as I read the story of Bartimaeus. I want my spiritual life to be like a blind man running, yet there is something that seems to hold my feet in their place like they are glued to the ground beneath me. I wonder, have I traded desperation for comfort? There was a time in my life when Jesus was all that mattered, and it was easy to cast off what little restraint I had as I sought Him. My spiritual life was defined by my hunger for His face, but somewhere along the line, I became more interested in His hand. Is it possible to renew my desire, or am I stuck here forever? The answer, of course, is an unequivocal no! I am not stuck, and neither are you! Have you not read, have you not heard, there is nothing too difficult for Him! He only limits Himself in proportion to your desire and surrender. The more you desire Him, the more He makes Himself known. I have found that desire is central to my life in Christ. To desire Him over what He can do for me, or to desire His intimate presence rather than my comfort, is the one thing that moves me forward in my pursuit of knowing Him.

RECOVERY

Recovery begins with a willingness to lose the power you have over your own life. I am always astonished by how unaware we can be when it comes to God, "What do you have for me?" is not the right question to ask of God. Recovery happens as we shift our priority from what we want God to do for us to what we can do in response to His question of how He can meet our needs. Admittedly, the differences in these statements seem insignificant, but the implications are huge. Stop for a moment to consider the exchange between Bartimaeus and Jesus. Bartimaeus began with a cry for mercy, and he continued to plead for mercy until he found himself face-to-face with Jesus. First, Bartimaeus offered his surrender with no strings attached. Once asked by Jesus what he wanted, he was able to reply. I know, just like you, that he wanted new eyes, but he began where we all must begin, with a correct understanding of who we are and who He is. He is the creator, and we are His creation. Please tell me how can creation presume to demand of the Creator. Yet, I see it all the time. People walk away from faith because someone they hold dear has died of old age. Reality check, my friend…No one gets out of that appointment! You cannot hold God responsible for the hurt you feel; no one gets a hall pass from death. You probably know someone who is living with resentment toward the church and God because the pastor did not live up to expectations or another church member maliciously mistreated someone. The point of all this is just this: when we enter into any relationship to have our own needs met first, we will always be hurt, even if that relationship is with God Himself. The gravitational pull of that kind of relationship is toward self-centered interests rather than mutual love. Remember what Paul wrote: *"Love doesn't demand its way."*[30] If we are to experience any real renewal with God, it begins with surrender and stays in that lane.

We too easily forget that this life, with all of its trials and tests, is the classroom that prepares us for our earthly and eternal assignment. Yes, I know we will rest from all our labors, but we were created with purpose, a creative intellect, and a drive to accomplish. I do not believe those will be erased when we step into eternity. There is so much more that awaits us that we cannot possibly understand or foresee on this side of our death. This I can assure you! You and I will not be sitting on a cloud, leisurely strumming a harp; there is more, so much more, and the weight of this life prepares us for the unfolding glory of the next. That, my friend, is the reason that we should pursue Jesus like a blind man running, casting off all that so easily hinders. He wants to do so much more in us than simply restoring blind eyes. He wants all of us, fully, unrestrained, surrendered in an ongoing partnership with Him. That partnership begins in the here and now, and it is meant to reveal God to others. That's our assignment on this side of eternity: to know Him and make Him known.

CHAPTER 6: RECOVERY

I wonder if the hard time you are going through is to prepare you for your next assignment. The merciful and gracious God is working to increase your capacity for what is next in this life and to prepare you for His presence in Eternity.

I believe with all my heart that is what Bartimaeus found that day. He got new eyes, but he also was being prepared for his ongoing assignment as part of God's household. That encounter with Jesus was the first of many encounters with God in relationship to life's hardships that would increase his capacity for future assignments. God began to replace all that was stolen from Bartimaeus, and He can do the same for you. In His presence, the thieving ends!

CHAPTER 7: CLARITY

"The people who walked in darkness have seen a great light; those who dwelt in a land of deep darkness, on them has light shone."[31]

CONFLICT

All the world is at war! And war rages in more places than some distant battlefield. Since the dawn of human history, a war has raged within and between each of us. Even those who assert that mankind is basically good have to admit that, from time to time, we are capable of the darkest kinds of evil. Sin is not a popular word, but it is a consistent reality for every person who resides on this planet. It is that simple three-letter word, sin, that is the instigator and sustainer of all the injustice the world experiences. Years ago, I attended a church conference in Dallas, Texas, where the host pastor said something that has stuck with me all these long years later. He said that the beginning of wisdom is to call something by its right name, and then he gave a most astounding example. He said that the right name for "neighbors" would be "conflict management." Humorous, but too often true!

The point is this: within my own lifetime, the church and the world have abandoned the word "sin" in favor of more benign and palatable words. But if we are to accurately understand the conflict that saturates the world, then we must call the problem by its right name...sin! Often, the popular opinion is to water down the words describing our sin while blaming some other person or institution or even a tangible thing for the injustice we see, but the truth is that sin lurks in each of us and is at the root of all injustice and suffering. At home and in the news media, we are reminded daily about how much injustice is experienced in the world. Is it any wonder that some people feel depressed, so imprisoned by forces beyond their control?

I have noticed that when people are willing to set aside their pride while taking an accurate inventory of their character, they can gain some freedom as they "call their sin by its right name." All sin tends to hide and camouflage itself so that it can survive to oppress another day. Its goal is to remain in control, so being rightly identified is counterproductive to continuing to hold people captive. I hope you understand by now that our enemy works hard to keep you in your secret prison. Things like addiction, self-serving control, especially narcissism, reshaping God into our preferred image, or a host of other, less obvious sins all need to be rightly identified, named, and then surrendered to our Lord Jesus.

Bartimaeus engaged Jesus because of an obvious physical defect, but I can assure you that more than eyes received mercy and grace that day. How do I know this? Bartimaeus, the "unfit son of filth," was human, and to be human is to be a captive to sin's sway. There is one other hint that shows more than eyes were healed. The scriptures say that *"he followed Jesus in the way."*[32] We have seen others healed by Jesus who celebrated their healing, but seldom does the Bible record that they followed Jesus. Bartimaeus may not have confessed his particular sins to Jesus at that moment, but he was not finished with Jesus, and Jesus was not yet finished with Bartimaeus. He needed more clarity as he rightly assessed his own need for Jesus' ever-new mercies.

RENEWED

What makes the story of Bartimaeus so spectacular is that the One who would free the blind, "unfit son of filth," would suffer and die on behalf of one so unworthy. The Cross was just over a week away, and that cross would put God Almighty in the valley of the shadow of death. His suffering validates our own, and the universal fact of human suffering only increases the glory and value of all that awaits those who put their full trust in the God who suffered. He showed us this through blind Bartimaeus. Jesus validates the most unworthy by inviting him into His presence, then goes even further by giving Bartimaeus new eyes and a new heart. Is it possible that Bartimaeus' blindness only intensifies and glorifies his newfound sight? If it is, then the same could be said about you. Your dark road is not something that any person would choose, and no person should have to bear what you have, but all that suffering and all that injustice will only increase the glory of your renewed life as you throw yourself into the arms of the Savior, Jesus! Trust the One who is Lord of all creation and is victorious over sin and death. Become Bartimaeus. Throw off all that can so easily hinder you. Trust Him, and run without concern about how others may see you. Meet the Savoir like a blind man running! Allow Jesus to do the work that you have been unable to complete.

    A renewed life is a spectacularly beautiful thing! The shattered pieces of that life have been reassembled and given value and new beauty. You are exactly like the Japanese art of *kintsugi*. If you are unfamiliar with this ancient practice, it is the art of repairing broken ceramics with gold, making the renewed dish more dazzling and more valued than the original. Take just a moment to look up *kintsugi* online, view some photographs, and then meditate on how much Christ's suffering and death have done to repair and beautify your life. In *kintsugi*, each repaired flaw is enhanced and beautified by the gold that bonds together each flaw and shattered piece. *Kintsugi* and God's Grace are all about embracing your flaws and imperfections because God has! He knows we are but dust but loves us more than we can fully comprehend this side of death. Oh, we have an idea of how deep His love runs because of the cross of Christ. We know the symbolism, we know the theology, and we have some personal revelation as we submit our lives to Jesus, the Christ, but full revelation is reserved for another day. Therefore, preparing your mind for action and being sober-minded, set your hope fully on the grace that will be brought to you at the revelation of Jesus Christ.[33] We will be perfected in His presence. Who knows? Perhaps we may look more like that *kintsugi* bowl that we have thought. It is certain that in His presence, we will see His scars and our renewed life, and then we will, without doubt, know that suffering has been glorified in His presence.

CHAPTER 7: CLARITY

THE TENSION OF IN-BETWEEN

Your conversion was not God's ultimate intention for your life! Your conversion and mine were simply the threshold for entering into a partnership with God almighty so that we might make Him known in the world around us. We were designed to live in a close, intimate relationship with Him in this life and the one to come. The reason this gets so blurred, so muddied, is the now and not-yet reality of the Gospel.

Often, very often, Jesus said that the kingdom of God was "at hand." At hand sounds very near, happening now, or at least very, very soon. Yet our calendars say that millennia have come and gone since Jesus uttered those words. Was He exaggerating, or was He just wrong? Did the Gospel writers embellish His words? What could He possibly mean by His "the Kingdom is at hand" statements? The answer is both complex and simple. The simplest answer is this: Jesus' entrance into history opened the door to the kingdom of God on Earth. And what He began is not yet finished. You know this in your own spiritual life! The Spirit of God has been deposited in you, but you also know that you are not yet fully completed in Christ, not this side of eternity. So, there is a tension we all must live with; it is the tension of "now I'm saved by the blood of Christ, but I am not yet fully glorified for the kingdom while I live on Earth." Is it any wonder that we can experience seasons of confusion and wandering? No! Because we live in the now and not yet of the kingdom. We are being prepared. We are being shaped by all that we must face in faith. The process of trusting God and surrendering to His sovereign hand is forming a glory for Christ that we have not considered. Be not ashamed of your life; God is using it to reveal a Glory in Jesus that will magnify God and His glorious Son.

We too easily forget that this life, with all of its trials and tests, is the classroom that prepares us for our eternal assignment. Yes, I know we will rest from all our labors, but we were created with purpose, a creative intellect, and a drive to use these. I do not believe that these will be erased when we step into eternity. There is so much more that awaits us that we cannot possibly understand or foresee on this side of our death. This I can assure you! You and I will not be sitting on a cloud, leisurely strumming a harp; there is more, so much more, and the weight of this life prepares us for the unfolding story of the next.

Take hold of hope, my friend! Your brokenness need not define you. It may be true that you have been known by a less-than-flattering label, just like Bartimaeus, but he found healing at the other end of his boldness. So can you!

ACCEPTANCE

If there is anything that the collision between Jesus and Bartimaeus teaches us, it is that even the most rejected, those declared unfit, can be fully accepted and restored. And it is time for you to accept your new identity in Christ! His work on the cross and His victory over the empty tomb must give you some hope in what He can do in you. Cast aside your impatience with how slowly He seems to be working a Bartimaeus-like miracle in your life! Again, my mind goes back to a moment when I was a student; our professor said the most astounding thing to our class. He said, "It takes the Sovereign Creator, you know, the One who can speak worlds into existence; it takes God thirty-three months to make a two-year-old child. God is not in a hurry, and perhaps you should be a bit more patient with yourself and with others." God is not through with you, and He is not through with those who are part of your life. Perhaps it's time to accept God's timing and pace. He is working to bring about glory through you for His own Son, our Savior, Jesus, the Christ! Your brokenness and your willingness to submit to His guiding hand, day by day, serve to reveal a glory that could not be revealed any other way. He has so much more for you than sitting in the dust at the side of Jericho's road. Leap to your feet, then run to Him as you accept His mercy and grace so freely given.

CHAPTER 8: FOLLOW

"I have faith in God. I don't have faith in something; I have faith in Someone." —Dr. George Bowker

INVITATION

Every person must choose the path that they will follow, and every one of us is invited to go on a quest to find God's heart. That spiritual journey is much more than a simple choice of aligning with a church or developing a religious worldview. The choice given to each of us is to literally know Jesus while following Him or to choose a path of our own making. I'm sorry to say there is no middle ground here. There are not multiple paths that lead to the same destination, as so many would have us now believe. The scriptures are full, from the first pages to the last, of people who were determined to make their way while insisting that God would approve of their chosen path. Yet, the same scriptures are clear that these missed the heart of God only to find themselves on the outside of glory while looking for glory. Here is how Jesus stated this principle:

CHAPTER 8: FOLLOW

"Not everyone who says to me, 'Lord, Lord,' will enter the kingdom of heaven, but the one who does the will of my Father who is in heaven. "On that day many will say to me, 'Lord, Lord, did we not prophesy in your name, and cast out demons in your name, and do many mighty works in your name?' And then will I declare to them, 'I never knew you; depart from me, you workers of lawlessness.'"[34]

In our current culture that values individual freedom above all else, this sounds unbelievably harsh and narrow. So, that would mean that the world's argument would sound something like this: "If Jesus is so good and loving, would He really have said something as intolerant as this? He must have meant something less harsh." Yet, He did say it! Read the rest of scripture, and you will find His words dovetail perfectly with the overall message of the Word of God. In fact, if you look closely at the argument that the world presents for more openness in interpreting the scriptures, you will find that it literally mirrors the argument that Satan used to ensnare Adam and Eve in the garden. So here we are, living in an era that has traveled full circle right back to Genesis chapter three, where everyone is tempted to question God's wisdom while fully trusting their own.

The writer of Hebrews gives us a clear and decisive warning about following our path. Here is how it is stated:

> Therefore, we must pay much closer attention to what we have heard, lest we drift away from it. For since the message declared by angels proved to be reliable, and every transgression or disobedience received a just retribution, how shall we escape if we neglect such a great salvation?[35]

Drift may well be the perfect word used to describe your spiritual life. Most of the time, people with great intentions are unaware of how they are drifting. Usually, as you think about your own life, you think you have done all the right things that help you maintain your spiritual standing. But this vein of thinking is concrete proof of your own drift. Anything that you do to guarantee your spiritual standing with God has moved from grace to effort. Simply put, it is Jesus plus something else. Jesus plus something always equals nothing. This small equation will always put us on a path of our own making, which will lead us off track in such small increments that we can be headed in the general direction but not on track. Clearly, drift is neither a right nor left turn; it is an imperceptible and casual movement that is just a little bit off course. This teaching found in Hebrews is echoed by the Spirit speaking through John in chapter two of Revelation. *"But I have this against you, that you have abandoned the love you had at first. Remember therefore from where you have fallen; repent, and do the works you did at first. If not, I will come to you and remove your lampstand from its place, unless you repent."*[36] I can say from personal experience that this may be the single most accurate indictment of present-day believers. I have drifted, growing complacent and satisfied with my nonchalant hunger for the heart of God. I believed that Jesus died for my sins, and I had at one point surrendered my life to Him, yet because I was managing my life in my own way, doing the right things in the right way, I had drifted into the ocean of no spiritual power, no real love for God, even as I kept plenty of that love for myself. I had gotten to the place where I was able to reduce God to a position of only meeting my desires when I wanted them. I desired God's hand rather than His face. I know that you understand this fundamental: when a relationship between two people is defined by what one can do for the other, that is no real relationship; it's a contract. Each time I read Hebrews or Revelation, I would cringe as I read those passages because I knew I had drifted off course. I wanted more because I felt so empty but had no idea how to find my way back. I was so far off course that I thought that this state must be acceptable, and all I needed to do was to hope that I could make it to the end of my life without feeling any emptier. What a sad and mirey place to exist! God, indeed, has more for us than just holding on until we cross over as we transition from this life to the next.

I had one thing working for me that helped me find my way back into a "first love" life with Jesus. It was this: I understood the law of grace. God's grace so saturates His creation that He tirelessly works to bring all humanity into a firsthand relationship with Him. His prevenient grace is never withdrawn! So, if I was feeling the desire for a renewed and enlivened relationship with Him, it was because He was drawing me! He was working on my behalf, and I just needed to respond to His invitation for a course correction and a deeper life. His prevenient grace is the secret to all my hunger, longing, seeking, and calling out. That grace exhibited in my longing for more of Him was the catalyst that sent me on a journey to rediscover His face, to hear His voice, and to long for His sanctifying presence. That same longing in your heart is not your own. It is the Spirit of the Living God drawing you into a more personal and intimate relationship with your Creator. We pursue God because He first puts the urge in us! Once again, I want to remind you that an invitation to leap to your feet and run full steam into the arms of Jesus is yours. How do you propose to respond? What will you do to regain that "first love" relationship?

Here are a few suggestions. They will vary from person to person and from situation to situation, but generally speaking, these should help guide you as you seek to follow Him.

PERSONHOOD

Have you noticed that in the era in which we live, we have almost forgotten that God is a person? But since He is a person, relationship can be cultivated. Just as you decide and then work to cultivate a relationship with another person, so too, you must decide to seek the heart of God and then do the work necessary to cultivate that relationship.

I have had a relationship with my best friend for more than forty-five years. It began with a simple invitation to a meal and then other moments of cultivating friendship. We have hiked, backpacked, camped, eaten thousands of meals, and spent countless hours together. In our case, we both had to decide for the other person, but in our pursuit of God, His decision was made before the foundation of the world. So, now the only decision that must be made is the one you must make. My relationship with any of the men I call friends does not just happen; they each made a decision and took corresponding actions.

God is not an ideal, or principal, or a force; He is a real person who, within the mighty depths of His person, thinks, feels, wills, enjoys, loves, and desires, and even suffers. His heart longs for you, and He is not through pursuing you. He will continue to call your name, and He will continue to fill your heart with a desire to know Him because He has created you for a relationship. The Westminster Catechism addresses this relationship when it asks the question: "What is the chief purpose of man?" and the answer comes: "To know God and enjoy Him forever."

But there is a paradox in this relationship, just as in any other you might have. To find God is not the end of the pursuit; it is just the beginning! The more we encounter Him, the more our hunger to know Him grows. The more that we "taste and see that He is good,"[37] the more we hunger and thirst for His satisfying depths. Is it any wonder that mere religion and religious behavior leave us feeling so empty? They are counterfeit relationships. He is a real person, and He can be found, but since He is already pursuing you, you must decide and then act, searching for Him. It can be done! One of my favorite Bible passages speaks to this seeking principle and calms my anxious heart because I intimately know all the reasons why He should not respond to my seeking. But in Isaiah, I find hope; *"I did not speak in secret, in a land of darkness; I did not say to the offspring of Jacob, 'Seek me in vain.' I the LORD speak the truth; I declare what is right."*[38] He has said, seek Me, and you will find Me. This is not some hidden and secret truth. No, He spoke this truth for all to hear. And He invited the offspring of Jacob, the deceiver, usurper, and cheater. Oh, how my heart sings. I am not cast off. I am invited! And so are you! Decide, then act. Begin to seek His heart today, and do not stop seeking—ever! Find a way to search out His heart. Make it a priority and make it a life-long pursuit!

PALMS DOWN

Part of the drift I experienced was because I was willing to release everything, palm down with one hand while holding tightly to something in my other. This partial surrender sent me into spiritual isolation and delusion. It's amazing to me how we do not understand that insisting that God do things our way or that He meets our self-centered demands will cloud and confuse our mind and spirit. Do you not understand that insisting that you get to keep what matters most to you is a form of idolatry and that a single decision will always open the door to more compromise, drift, and faulty spiritual pursuits? The invitation to follow is not an invitation to the comfortable and convenient. Truly following God takes an unencumbered life, one in which, one by one, the things that own you are surrendered with palms turned down.

Bartimaeus did this when he cast aside all that had been his security so that he could move unencumbered into Jesus' presence. Then, as he faced his Savior and Healer, his heart was so transformed that he wanted more and more of the unfathomable depths of our Savior. He left behind the life that he had known for so long so that he could follow Jesus in the way.

THE TENACIOUS VOICE

Becoming lost while on foot in the forest or the desert is a frightening experience for anyone. Losing track of all known landmarks or known paths only adds disorientation to the already confused mind. The heart begins to race, and the mind and eyes search for anything that might help get back on track. But you just can't seem to make the necessary adjustments that can help inform you of your location. Panic can take over, causing you to make even more life-threatening mistakes. Even in this age of satellites and hand-held GPS instruments, people still get lost and sometimes pay for their mistakes with their lives. No one likes to read these kinds of news stories because we know that there are so many resources available to help guide one in the wilderness, so our hearts break over such a sad story of loss. Maps, GPS, adequate water, and supplies can get us home after wandering around unfamiliar paths, just as God's voice is necessary for a safe spiritual journey.

God is speaking! He did not speak, then sat back, waiting to see what His words would do. The scriptures are clear: they do not say that He spoke. No, they say that He speaks and is actively involved. Jesus said, "My Father is working until now, and I am working."[39] The Father and His Son have not acted and then become uninvolved. No! They are working, present tense, and since they are working, they are also speaking—to you! His word spoken from the foundation of the world is still living and active and present for each of us. The writer of Hebrews said it this way: *"For the word of God is living and active, sharper than any two-edged sword, piercing to the division of soul and of spirit, of joints and of marrow, and discerning the thoughts and intentions of the heart."*[40] The scriptures are not dry, dusty, or outdated; they are living and active, ready and waiting for you to engage yourself with them. Open the scriptures, read and meditate, pray over them, and let them become a guide for your prayers. Don't ever be that Christian who carries his Bible into church and then leaves it in the car the rest of the week. God is speaking, and the primary way He is speaking to you is through His Word.

FOLLOW

Bartimaeus already has shown us that unrestrained hunger for Jesus can transform all forms of brokenness, but he also demonstrates one other spiritual principle we all must own. He stepped onto the road that leads out of his familiar Jericho so that he could follow his Savior. So, too, we must actively follow Jesus in the way. We must turn our backs on the life that has kept us imprisoned, blinded, and begging by the side of a dusty road of our own making. Why would anyone want to remain in a place that has weighed down their life to the point of desperation? Yet sadly, many make just that choice. Following the Savoir requires that we leave behind the familiar and comfortable because we, like Bartimaeus, recognize what sin and willfulness have cost us. Tell me please, why are we so hesitant? Why do we choose our own path rather than the one that the Savior has marked out for us?

- CHAPTER 8: FOLLOW -

Bartimaeus knew the road that led from his dwelling place to his spot reserved for begging, but he was fully unfamiliar with the road beyond that point. The road leading to Jerusalem was not known as it presented itself to him in new, exciting, and yet terrifying ways. Isn't that the way all new opportunities work? They are both exhilarating and fearsome at the same time. Too often, when it comes to new spiritual adventures, we hesitate and, at times, backtrack because of the fearsome unknown laid out before us. And yet the scriptures are clear. Bartimaeus found his courage to follow Jesus. He had no idea what lay ahead; he had no clue what he would encounter, but at this moment, fear and uncertainty did not matter. All he knew was that there was One who met his need and invited him into a form of freedom that was too precious to lose.

My friend, it is time to follow! Get your eyes off the "what-ifs" and all the baggage that you must cast off to the side of the road instead, and fix your gaze fully on Jesus, who is the initiator and sustainer of your life and salvation. Yours is to follow and stay as close to Jesus as possible because, in His presence, all things are made new!

CHAPTER 9:
GRACE AND GRIEF

> Sacrament: A Christian sign or symbol in which a sacred or spiritual power is transmitted through material elements viewed as channels of divine grace.

GRACE AND GRIEF

It has been said that to love is to open oneself to grief because one cannot love without some form of loss. Death separates, pain dissipates, and grief hides. Have you noticed that grief always follows close behind grace? Every high and exuberant season is followed by another one of testing. We live in a world governed by cycles; seasons give way to seasons, just as birth gives itself over to death. The same could be said of Bartimaeus. His healing and the exuberant road that led to Jerusalem eventually made its way to Golgotha. New eyes and a new heart kept him on the road that he used to make his living, but this time, instead of begging, he was following the Healer/Savior, Jesus. He followed Jesus in the way[41], which means that he saw and felt the Triumphant Entry. All of Jerusalem turned out to verify what Bartimaeus had just experienced. How exhilarating that must have been!

CHAPTER 9: GRACE AND GRIEF

Not only had he found his Savior and Healer, but his choice to move from invisibility to visibility was being confirmed by almost everybody. In his initial encounter with the Lord, he had referred to Jesus as the "Son of David," a military and messianic term, and now everything he hoped for seemed to be coming true. The crowd was solidly affirming the prophet from Galilee. Could it be true that Jesus would be the one who would deliver Israel from oppression, ushering in a new age of blessing?

We know the rest of the story; we have the advantage of an accurate look back, but no one in that crowd had that advantage. They had scriptural prophecies at the moment they were living, so their vision was fairly myopic. As far as they could see, everything seemed to be leading them to a pleasant and hope-filled future, yet that was not the case. We know that by the end of that week, the emotional and political tide had shifted, and all the disciples who followed Jesus would find themselves scattered, hopeless, and living in fear. We know that Jesus, the perfect, spotless lamb of God, would suffer a torturous death and be buried. We know that all this was for the good of everyone who finds their sins forgiven because of His willingness to lay down His life for you, me, and every Bartimaeus crazy enough to trust His mighty work on the cross. We know the "rest of the story": they did not have that advantage; they had only what their eyes could see and their hearts feel.

THE SACRAMENT OF THE ROAD

I hope you see the correlation between what Jesus's disciples experienced and your own life. What begins as a season of great hope and exhilaration often morphs into a season of questions and days that feel utterly hopeless. Grace is often followed by grief. The question you and Bartimaeus must answer is, what will you do when the bottom drops out of what you expected to be deliverance?

Nothing, but nothing, will get your full attention like pain. Physical pain will imprison you, but emotional/spiritual pain can, too. If allowed to have its way, it will confuse, distract, and orient you toward the wrong things. While pain feels unique and individual, it is the great equalizer, touching virtually everyone. No one outruns or hides from pain. It will find you. When it does, you will very likely feel abandoned and alone because, in this dark place, God's presence is often undetectable, and His voice seems to be silenced. Pain will steal what seems to matter most, but it can also strip away all pretense and delusion while calling you to embrace what matters. Pain has the power to help you brush away all that can hinder you in your pursuit of God's heart and can give you clearer vision.

For Bartimaeus and the disciples, that road out of Jericho became a sacramental road because a sacrament is an external expression of the inward work of God's grace. For all those whose trust in Jesus was solid, the journey from Jericho to Golgotha formed the first sacramental journey that would transform casual adherents into disciples who would live and die as Jesus did. We are not told in scripture about what happened to Bartimaeus, only that he followed Jesus in the way. We don't know how Bartimaeus reacted to the cross that fateful Friday or if he found out about the empty tomb on Sunday. We don't know if he abandoned faith like so many others who saw Jesus' death as a permanent, irreversible event or if he remained with the disciples. That road was the first test of faith among many because that is how life works. Victory is followed by grief; then we are tested and refined in preparation for the next victory and loss. Like driving through mountains followed by valleys, victory, and hope are followed by loss and grief. We are not told if Bartimaeus was overwhelmed by defeat at the foot of the cross or if he found his way to faith again after the disciples began their ministry. Whatever happened, I am convinced that his faith held firm through the testing because he followed Jesus on the way.[42] That simple statement sets a course that is ongoing. Even if he found himself full of doubts and unanswerable questions following the Cross, so did the disciples. They found their way back and then set the world ablaze with truth and light.

Can the same be said of you? You have been tested, but does your passion for Him remain? Will you continue to throw off all restraint to run to Him, even when the road is bleak? The reason I ask this is that I have observed and experienced for myself an odd response to victory. Often, very often, when we cry out to God to relieve some form of personal suffering, miraculously, He answers. Our immediate response is to celebrate and praise His name. But eventually, we return to our old patterns and dangerous choices, precipitating a new season of desperate need and of calling out for relief. Then God answers our payers once again. Cycle upon cycle of blessing and want. Is this really how He intends for us to live? I don't believe that for a moment, and that is why I believe that the road from Jericho to Golgotha is so important. Because the road does not end at the Cross; it actually begins there! Following Jesus "in the way" from your Jericho to Golgotha is the threshold for entering into grace. The Cross is the station where your debt is paid, but at the empty tomb, life

CHAPTER 9: GRACE AND GRIEF

and hope are poured out on you. This is where real life begins and where strength to continue "in the way" is imparted to you.

I asked this earlier, but I feel I must ask again. Is it possible that all you have been through, especially the painful parts of your life, has been a sacrament intended to glorify God and prepare you for your assignment? Is the road in which you travel, following Jesus in the way, a sacramental road of both pain and victory? Is He leading you to a greater glory? That's what the sacramental road is intended to do. Glorify God by showing others that if He can get you through all your "stuff," then He can help them, too. Your journey is not just for you! Your pain and victory are not to be hoarded or worn like military medals so that people notice your accomplishments. No, your struggles are for God's glory and the benefit of others.

When will you stop blaming your circumstances, your failures, or your weakness for where you have been forced to beg? Do what Bartimaeus did! Run like one who has nothing left to lose into the arms of Jesus. Trust Him to do the work necessary to heal your hurt, then set the course of your life upon the sacramental road as you "follow Him in the way." Do you not see, the healing of Bartimaeus' eyes put him on a long road of continual transformation? So too is your healing! Praise the

Lord for your sacramental road.

With all this in mind, the question arises: What can I expect to find along my sacramental road? How will my life be different as I follow Jesus in the way? The next chapter addresses these very questions. Read on...

CHAPTER 10: EXPECTATIONS

> "The Son of God suffered unto death, not that men might not suffer, but that their sufferings might be like His."[43]
>
> —George MacDonald

EXPECTATIONS ARE POWERFUL

Expectations are very powerful things; they can help you lead you to unimaginable heights, or they can imprison you in the dark cell of disappointment and frustration. Expectations can cement a relationship, or they can be the nuclear blast that destroys it. In every part of our lives, expectations govern how we engage with the world and those we love. Your expectations will even influence how you approach and relate to God. When your expectations are met, you feel like you are on top of the world and that you can do no wrong, but when they are unmet, it can feel like hell is unleashed. Expectations are very powerful things!

By now, I hope that you understand that we, each of us, are flawed and broken in many ways, meaning we approach or pursue God with faulty and flawed assumptions and expectations. It is a good thing that He is rich in mercy and grace! He remembers that we are but dust and incapable of approaching Him with anything that resembles perfection. That is precisely why the "son of filth" could run to Him just outside Jericho. And that is why He allowed Bartimaeus' flawed Messianic view and why He is so open to you and me. His mercy and grace overwhelm our brokenness; bless His holy name! Still, our imperfect expectations and assumptions can add unnecessary weight and spiritual detours to our journey, causing us to mistake the work of the Father for something that it is not. A perfect example of this is found in John 9. The disciples had a faulty assumption about a blind man, asking Jesus, "Who sinned, this man or his parents?"[44] The answer was: neither this man nor his parents, you misunderstand the heart of God. I have had seasons in my life, and I'm sure you have too, when we misunderstood God's heart. Our expectations, both physical and spiritual, were not met, so we entered that dull gray of uncertainty and insecurity. If our expectations are unaddressed, they will always lead us into the dry desert of estranged Father/child relationship. I know firsthand how easy it is to allow insecurity in me, causing me to neglect my relationship with God. It's natural, don't you think, for us to hide just like Adam and Eve did when they fell from grace. Hiding feels so much safer than facing a Holy God, but you and I both know that hiding and neglecting our relationship with God does nothing to build security within us. If it does anything, it makes us even more insecure and uncertain. Instead, we need to square our shoulders and take personal responsibility for our actions and attitudes. Then as we humbly submit to God's discipline, He renews our spirit as He sets us on a secure path back to Himself. You and I can expect that when we seek Him with all our hearts, we will find Him and all that goes with knowing Him personally.

What else can we expect to find on the sacramental road we each travel?

EXPECT TRIALS, TROUBLES, AND TEMPTATIONS

The Apostle Peter said it best when he wrote in his first epistle: Don't be surprised when life hurts you. Here is how he said it: *"Beloved, do not be surprised at the fiery trial when it comes upon you to test you, as though something strange were happening to you."*[45] Pain, testing, and temptations are to be expected this side of eternity, no exceptions! As I reflect on my life, I'm a bit taken aback by how often I have been surprised by trials that came my way. It is no secret that the human race craves stability and comfort while expecting stability to be the norm. So, we often treat God as if He were our "Get out of jail free" card, believing that as we surrender our lives to Him, He keeps us from all harm, all disasters, and trials. But rather than getting us out of trials and temptations, every time they come our way, he desires to strengthen us through them.

Have you noticed that you can generally divide trials into three different categories? The first category could be labeled "Cause and Effect." We understand this principle in the natural world. It works this way: If you were to leap from the roof of your house without any safety equipment to cushion your fall, you would end up with broken bones and likely other complications from such a foolish act. Cause and Effect trials come our way when we do something stupid or wrong that has consequences. Just as ignoring or minimizing the law of gravity carries consequences, so does ignoring or minimizing any other natural law or spiritual law. Choosing to bypass local laws can land you in jail whether you are a Christian or not. We make choices every day, and there are times when some of the choices we make are not as stellar as they should be; it's part of the human condition to make some poor choices. The consequences of your choices are not someone else's way to oppress you, it

CHAPTER 10: EXPECTATIONS

was your choice, and some choices carry hard consequences. Own your choices and face their consequences.

Since all of life is tied to the spiritual, there are spiritual ramifications to all our choices. Temptations that we choose to follow fall into this cause-and-effect category; here is why. As we give in to temptations, we choose to move incrementally away from God's best, choosing our own desires instead. We are commanded in scripture to carefully nurture the Spirit of God who has been deposited in us. The scriptures say it this way. *"And do not grieve the Holy Spirit of God, by whom you were sealed for the day of redemption."*[46] And this passage from another of Paul's epistles: *"Do not quench the Spirit."*[47] We quench the Spirit when we do what is wrong, and we grieve the Spirit when we don't do what is right. I know that this can sound like I'm splitting hairs, but these two choices are among the most common cause-and-effect moments in the life of a Christian that, if left unattended, can cause a chilling of the heart and spiritual amnesia. Each choice we make that is for self rather than for the heart of God dulls our spiritual memory and cools our heart toward God. Carefully guard your spirit, and the Spirit will carefully guard you.

The second kind of trial that we can face is suffering as Christians. John recorded the words of Jesus so that we would not be caught unaware. Remember the word that I said to you: If they persecuted me, they will also persecute you. If they kept my word, they will also keep yours. *"But all these things they will do to you on account of my name, because they do not know him who sent me."*[48] This is the kind of suffering or trial that comes to us simply because we identify with Jesus Christ. Sometimes, it is at the hand of others who resent the name of Jesus. Other times it is by the permissive will of God to test and prove our faith. Just read the book of Job to get a full picture of this.

But more often than the first two kinds of trials and suffering, we will experience a third type: Unexplained Trials. This kind of suffering seems to make no sense because it is not a result of a selfish action or for the testing of your faith; although it may test that faith, it just happens because the world we live in is broken. One of the best scriptural examples of this kind of trail is David's *Ziklag*. Read 1 Samuel 27 and 29–30, three chapters that tell the story of how David and his men lost their homes and families while they were doing their best to serve God. If you have not read through this part of the Bible, spoiler alert; they regain their families and all that they cared about. But the loss and pain they experienced seemed to come from nowhere and felt completely meaningless and overwhelming. What makes this story so valuable for us is how David responded to his multiple losses. And David was greatly distressed, for the people spoke of stoning him because all the people were bitter in soul, each for his sons and daughters. *"But David strengthened himself in the LORD his God."*[49] This statement means that David got alone for the singular purpose of worshiping God one-on-one. Personal and corporate worship will get you through the worst of trials, and both are vital to your ongoing life in Christ. Personal worship will help you cling to the heart of God, while corporate worship will ground you in kingdom relationships. **More worship, less playing the victim!**

EXPECT MERCY AND GRACE

One of my favorite Bible passages to read when I'm feeling a bit vulnerable is found in Exodus chapter 34.

> The LORD passed before him and proclaimed, "The LORD, the LORD, a God merciful and gracious, slow to anger, and abounding in steadfast love and faithfulness, keeping steadfast love for thousands, forgiving iniquity and transgression and sin, but who will by no means clear the guilty…"[50]

Did you notice that this self-disclosure from God-Almighty begins with Mercy and Grace, then moves on to loving patience, faithfulness, and steadfast love? Judgment and justice are not ignored or dismissed, but mercy and grace lead God's character even as He judges; bless His holy name! No wonder Bartimaeus could run with such confidence. Mercy and grace awaited him. It is no mystery why he would choose to follow Jesus in the way. All the mercy and grace he could desire was housed in the person of Jesus. No one who has received as much as he had would turn their back to walk their own track. But all of this does not guarantee that the road will be easy or comfortable.

Our sacramental road can be fraught with dangers, disappointments, and detours, but one thing remains fixed in our spinning and wobbly world: the character of God! No matter where our road leads, God is present, and His grace and mercy never dissipate. All the grace you need for the day has already been applied before you even opened your eyes this morning. This does not mean that today will be easy or comfortable, but it does mean that every resource you will need has been effectively gathered for you. All that is needed from you is to face your Savior and trust Him as you follow Him in the way. **God's character is fixed! Quiet your worry.**

CHAPTER 10: EXPECTATIONS

EXPECT TO ENCOUNTER GOD ALMIGHTY

"You will seek me and find me when you seek me with all your heart. I will be found by you, declares the Lord..."[51]

"And without faith it is impossible to please him, for whoever would draw near to God must believe that he exists and that he rewards those who seek him."[52]

He has not spoken in secret. He has not hidden Himself, and He has promised that if you do seek Him, you will find Him. There is not some complicated formula here; there is no mysterious, unreadable treasure map. He, who is the Author of Life and the First Source of all creation, has invited each of us into a guaranteed relationship if we simply search out His heart. By now, you should know that He is available to anyone, no matter how checkered their past may be. By now, you should know that you cannot expect success in this quest if you dictate the conditions of the relationship. You must throw off all that weighs you down and roots you to your past. If you can do this, then a relationship with the Almighty is a given. The reason that I'm so confident in this is that His Prevenient Grace has drawn you, and if you follow through on His invitation, He will keep His promise. God keeps His word. **Stop analyzing, start trusting, and keep searching.**

EXPECT WORSHIP TO BE YOUR NEW NORMAL

Encountering the living God will always lead one to bow low in worship. You may answer that you do that every Sunday morning, without fail, but authentic worship is more than showing up at church and singing a few hymns or worship songs. Worship is meant to be practiced on a personal level that prepares you for the corporate level. That means that you are meant to practice worship at home, and I would challenge you with this: daily devotions are not fully worship. That is unless you close the devotional book, set down your coffee, and then turn to face God one-on-one while telling Him what makes Him so unique, special, and your personal choice. Authentic private worship is personal, and it is God-centered. I once heard a children's pastor explain the complicated subject of worship to the children she was teaching. She said, "Worship is thinking and speaking, on purpose, about God only." This is a brilliant definition of worship! If you can make something fully understandable to children, then you have clarity that is foundational for everyone.

Know this: as you throw off all those restraints, as you leap to your feet while running into the arms of your Savior, then you repeat this action as often as you can, your daily time with Him will take on new dimensions of worship. Think about it: when you encounter the Living God, worship is the natural response. The seraphim who dwell in the presence of God can't help themselves: "And the four living creatures, each of them with six wings, are full of eyes all around and within, and day and night they never cease to say, *'Holy, holy, holy, is the Lord God Almighty, who was and is and is to come!'*"[53] When every patriarch and prophet found themselves in the Presence, they all fell to their faces and worshiped. Worship is a natural outcome of a deepening life in Christ, but it must be chosen, practiced, and then pursued. Drawing near to Jesus will create within you a longing to worship, but it does not come easily on this side of heaven. I can personally attest that worship that puts you in God's presence takes practice because we are so very busy and our minds are so full of other things. To discipline your mind and your heart to set these aside for a time of worship takes commitment and ongoing practice. But trust me, all saints who have developed this spiritual discipline will tell you that it is so worth every effort. Don't let feelings of failure or missed days rob you of the desire to stay at it. There is a reason that in the days of the Judges, there were Schools of Prophets. This kind of life must be learned and practiced. Worship, authentic worship, begins at home so that the church is prepared for authentic, God-centered worship each Sunday.

EXPECT AN ETERNAL REWARD

This life and all its trappings are not all that there is for one who believes in the life, death, and resurrection of Jesus, our Lord. We are made as physical and spiritual beings who are intended to live in the presence of their Creator. Everything we hold dear in this life is meant to fade and die so that real, unfading, and undying life takes its place. Heavenly mansions and streets of gold will be nice, but are they really what makes eternity so special? No, of course not! Family and friends wait for us, and for that, I'm very happy, but again, as good as that will be, they are not what will make life eternal so spectacular. I promise you that your attention will be owned by Jesus Christ and His Father. To be in their presence, to gaze upon their majesty will be our great and precious reward. To worship in His presence will be a reward of the highest order since all that veils our senses here will be removed there. To have our original design restored will out-pace and out-strip all that we think makes this life so spectacular. All this and some more await us on the other side of this life, so make this life count. What you began here will follow you into eternity.

CHAPTER 10: EXPECTATIONS

EXPECT MORE OF HIM, LESS OF YOU

Your sacramental road is meant to move you closer and closer to Jesus, and it will if you simply seek Him with all your heart and if you worship in private and with others. If you can find the courage to unpin your past and embrace your Savior without reservation, He will increase His presence and strength in you. You are invited into so much more than you have had. Make your choice today, and live all your life like a blind man running! You are invited to a renewed life in Christ.

EPILOGUE: TRAVELING ON YOUR JERICHO ROAD

"Let us then with confidence draw near to the throne of grace, that we may receive mercy and find grace to help in time of need."[54]

Being inspired by the story of Bartimaeus and then living your renewed life in Christ are two distinctly different things. Inspiration can fuel your passions, but to get anywhere, that fuel must be supplemented by feet that carry you forward on your Jericho Road. It has been said that good intentions get you nowhere; it is momentum and direction that get you to your goal. You can think all the good thoughts you want to think, or you can draw all the schematics and plans needed for a building project, but drawings and schematics are never mistaken for the actual building, and thinking good thoughts is not the same as meeting your goal. It's only logical. To build yourself a home, you must gather all the materials needed for its completion. Then, following the building plans, you must work until the building is finished. The same can be said for your renewed and growing life in Christ; plans must be made and then followed. So, where do you go from here? Where and how do you start? How can you put your inspiration to work? May I suggest you do what Bartimaeus did? Throw off all that restrains you so that you can pursue Jesus like a blind man running. Here are a few practical suggestions to help as you renew your journey with Jesus.

ENTERING IN HOPE: HOLD TIGHTLY TO HOPE

Call it biorhythms, or a lack of sleep, or chalk it up to stress, but there are simply some days that we must stand firm and secure in nothing but the promise and oath of God, knowing that He can't lie. He has secured your life and soul with the steadfast anchor of His immutable promises. Take hold of hope, oh my soul! You have a strong refuge in the time of any storm. Your resources may have dried up or have been forcibly taken, but He remains seated in the Heavens, and He continues His sovereign rule. Life may seem futile and heavier than you can possibly bear, but His words and promises concerning you have not failed. You do not seek Him in vain! Take hold of hope, oh my soul! Jesus entered the Holy of Holies on your behalf by presenting his own body as the perfect sacrifice to meet all your needs and to secure God's promises for you. Jesus offered for all time one sacrifice for sin, and He is making forever-complete all who put their full weight of trust in Him. Glory to God; what He has said is true and cannot change! Remember, hold on to these truths as you enter into a pursuit of His heart because some days are just hard.

- You are redeemed by His blood.
- You are healed by the stripes He bore in His own body.
- You are a child of God and the Bride of the Lamb, destined for an eternal reward.
- Peace is yours, and comfort is granted to you so that you may comfort others.
- He is present, and He is more faithful than any other person you have met.
- He has promised to bear you up when your strength is failing, and He directs, even re-directs, your footsteps so that you may find your way to your heavenly home.
- He works to help you fulfill your destiny, and He equips you to help others find theirs.

You are more than your brokenness, and you are lifted higher than your failures. Why? Because His promises are sure, and the work He did through Jesus for you is an anchor that can hold you steady in any storm. Hold tightly to hope! He has redeemed you from destruction. He has satisfied your life with good things, and He has crowned you with tender mercies and loving-kindness.[55] Hold tightly to hope!

As important as holding to hope is, there is one more thing that you must hold on to as you enter into your pursuit of God. It is this. Desire!

DESIRE

Desire for a thing will keep you moving toward it; mountaineers prove this each time they summit impossibly high mountain peaks. It does not take a lot of observation to note that desire drives all humanity. It was infused in us at our creation. If it was not, the enemy would not have been so successful in the Garden with Adam and Eve. He played to their sense of desire for significance to the ruin of all of God's creation. Yet…Jesus spoke powerfully and clearly about the redemption of our whole nature, including our desire.

If desire is such a large part of what drives you, then desire for Him can be one key that unlocks the power of your quiet time. When you come to your quiet time, the most important thing you can bring is your desire! Remember that. The Lord respects your freedom and is unwilling to force anything "unwanted" on you. He will enter into your life to the extent that you believe is possible and as far as you invite Him in. Your desire for Him, rather than His answers, will draw you into His very presence and will open the door to greater intimacy and spiritual effectiveness. Openness and desire will lead you to new vistas of knowing and enjoying God. The Apostle Paul said it this way:

> [...] that you, being rooted and grounded in love, may have strength to comprehend with all the saints what is the breadth and length and height and depth, and to know the love of Christ that surpasses knowledge, that you may be filled with all the fullness of God.[56]

Bring your desire, your singular desire, to your time of prayer and meditation. Stay at it! Keep seeking, keep desiring Him, and you will find Him in ways that you never thought possible. Bring your white-hot and singular desire for Him to your prayer time, then hold on. He will give you exactly what you desire and all that you believe is possible.

TRAVELING ON, OR DISCIPLINES FOR THE INNER LIFE
PRAYER: BREATHING OUT

Years ago, I had the privilege of standing at the headwaters of the Metolius River in Oregon. It is a remarkable thing to see. It begins as a small creek streaming up from underground, narrow enough that a person could jump from one side to the other if they wanted to. But if you go just a few yards downstream, that small creek becomes a strong, deep, and wide stream. Then, just a bit farther along, it becomes a deep and rushing river that is world-famous for its trout fishing. Almost imperceptible at its fountainhead, it grows and expands as it travels toward the Pacific Ocean. The Metolius River is a perfect picture of prayer. What begins as a small, often neglected discipline can become an unstoppable force, just like a mighty river.

For the Christian prayer is as necessary as breathing is to maintain life. But unlike breathing, which is governed by our nervous system, prayer is a practiced discipline, and like all disciplines, it grows and matures with practice. The problem I have noticed from my own life is that church leadership and families just assume that you know how to pray. Prayer is one of those spiritual disciplines that we all would like to improve, and while there are plenty of good books written on the subject of prayer, generally, we just hope that we get better at it without much study or a concrete improvement plan. We pray today; then we pray again the next day. So, like days that seem to blend into the next, our prayers seem to be one long continuum of asking for the same things. We know that we are to pray continually, but we sense that we may be missing something and wonder if there may be more. So, secretly, we question, "Could it be that everything I know about prayer is not all that God has for me?" Is it possible that you and I will spend our entire adult life missing the real power and purpose of prayer? Oh, I hope not! I want more. I want to pray like the Apostle Paul, who regularly prayed for Heaven to invade Earth. I want an effective prayer life that prays for large, heaven-moving things, and I want to know the intimacy of Jesus' literal presence while I'm on my knees.

I want to set aside my small and puny list of "feed me, protect me, bless me, and all those I love." These things are important, but if they are the entire focus of prayer, well then, I'd say we are missing something that the Apostles found. Pause for just a moment to consider these words written by Paul the Apostle:

> [...] we have not ceased to pray for you, asking that you may be filled with the knowledge of his will in all spiritual wisdom and understanding, so as to walk in a manner worthy of the Lord, fully pleasing to him: bearing fruit in every good work and increasing in the knowledge of God; being strengthened with all power, according to his glorious might, for all endurance and patience with joy...[57]

Sit with and meditate on the mighty weight of that prayer. That is a "Heaven Invading Earth" kind of prayer! Let it sink deeply into your heart. Now, think about how often your prayers run on that track. I would wager, not often. I believe that one of the reasons we don't often pray like that is that we, at our core, don't expect God to do things like that. We do expect that He is more skilled at blessing meals and protecting our kids or handing out traveling mercies, so we limit our prayers to what we expect that He is willing to do. O Lord, have mercy!

So, how do we move from where we are to where we long to be? There are a few steps we can take and a couple of attitudes that must be cultivated.

STEP ONE

This is where you begin, and I want you to know that this step is actually the easiest of all: pray. But…you must follow Jesus' teaching to find a private place that is dedicated to your time with Him. I know our lives are full of obligations, family, and so, so many other things, but I promise you that if you figure out how to begin here, prayer will begin to open its vistas to you. Step one: Get alone with God.

STEP TWO

Step two is very practical here: you read, study, and seek deep counsel on how to pray. Find a saint who is "higher up, further in" than you who is willing to be your mentor. Anything written on prayer by E. M. Bounds, Timothy Keller, or the book *The Valley of Vision* will deepen what you currently know. Step two: Seek expert guidance.

STEP THREE

Form a written plan for deepening your prayer life. You know the old adage, "You will hit nothing unless you aim." Pick a target, stay focused, and stay at it. What you are seeking will not come overnight or even next month! This is where the two attitudes come into play. The first attitude to cultivate is hunger. This cannot be overstated. You must develop a sort of holy discontent with where you are in your prayer life. Please don't settle for what you have; yearn for more in prayer. The second attitude to cultivate is expectation. One of the reasons our prayers seem so ineffective is that we don't fully expect the Lord to follow through for us. Hunger and expectations must align! The convergence of the two takes time, patience, and enduring in the faith. But I promise that you will find that you will be living out that prayer found above as you allow hunger to have its place in your prayers.

QUIET REFLECTION: BREATHING IN

I believe it was G. K. Chesterton who said, "God speaks, and nye onto incessantly." He does not lack for words or actions, and He does not lack in interaction with you. We are all able to say that He is present and actively involved with us, but my observation is that we often miss His voice found in the mundane nature of life. We are often so caught up in our routines and agendas that with our "heads down," we press ahead to get our work done or to own our leisure time. Yes, both at work and at leisure, we strive to manage life effectively. The problem is that often this focus on managing so much of life impedes our ability to clearly hear God's voice. This is why developing an intentional quiet space in our routine matters so much. We need to tune our ears to His voice because He has so much to say to His children. He speaks through the Scriptures. They are, after all, the Living Word of God. Sometimes the Spirit shouts, sometimes He whispers, but always He speaks His immeasurable love and patience toward us through the scriptures. They are to us a light and an effective guide. Have you noticed how close He is in your moments of temptation, providing the needed roadblock or interaction of a friend? Even in small moments that keep us on His appointed track, it is His loving voice saying, "Hold steady, my child." In our sorrow and loss, He speaks in the most intimate ways because He knows how desperately our hearts ache. The embrace of a friend or the card delivered to the mailbox on just the right day. The song on the radio or the daily devotion that speaks to our needs are not random happenstance; they are His comforting voice. Train your ears to hear His voice! All those little moments that grab your heart and mind…could they be the whisper of the Father speaking his love for you? Of course they are!

READ FOR TRANSFORMATION

Dr. Howard Hendricks said it best: "The Bible was not given to satisfy your curiosity, but to transform your life." Filling notebooks with Bible trivia will increase your head knowledge, but it does little to reshape your life. Since the Word of God is "living and active," it is not to be treated as anything less than that. But how do you approach the Word for transformation? I suggest these as basics.

- Begin with prayer. Open your Bible, but before you begin to read, pause and pray for clarity and the ability to hear God's voice. Ask for eyes to see and ears to hear; He is still speaking through His Word, and His desire is your transformation.
- Consider a journal. I realize that this is not for everyone. I certainly thought that I was exempt from this practice, but to my surprise, it has enhanced my Bible reading.
- Find trustworthy resources. Good commentaries and Bible dictionaries help in understanding difficult Bible texts. Do some research, then buy.
- Finish with prayer. Review your reading with the Lord, then listen.

FASTING: HUMBLING YOURSELF BEFORE THE LORD

Fasting is not a subject that many of us want to discuss these days. We do like our comfort a bit too much, so self-denial does not fall on eager ears. Yet fasting has been a regular practice of the saints for ages. Is it an outmoded, antiquated idea and practice, or can the saint in the twenty-first century gain something significant spiritually as he embraces this practice of fasting? I believe the answer to that question is a firm yes!

But too often, far too often, we treat fasting like some magic formula that backs God into a corner, forcing Him or persuading Him to meet our needs in the way we have prescribed. I have done this. I'll bet you have too. "I have fasted; now I will get my preferred answer." And when the fasting prayer is not answered, we give up. "Why fast? God didn't answer my prayer," we say without really considering our true motivations. Ezra and all other biblical leaders knew that fasting was not about securing what they wanted but for preparation and position. I have learned that these are the two compelling reasons we should never give up the practice. Other than fasting, there is no spiritual discipline that will reveal what's going on at your center or reveal it more vividly.

We fast to regain proper position. God alone is above all things, including our own needs. He is sovereign, and we too often treat Him as if we occupy His position. Fasting humbles us, giving us a clear picture of who we are and who He is. Fasting repositions my heart to align my heart to match His.

We fast to prepare our will to match His. Fasting is about seeking God's direction, not dictating my own. This discipline requires me to set aside my list so that I may find his. I prepare spiritually before I move physically. (To find some practical instructions for fasting, read Richard Foster's *Celebration of Discipline*.)

FINDING YOUR STRIDE

The road you are to travel is uniquely yours, but there are some common steps and common traits every believer should share. These are meant to help you gauge yourself throughout your journey, and they can help you as you seek Godly companions on your journey. Jesus highlighted thirteen of these traits as He spoke to the five thousand seated on a hillside in Galilee. Jesus often compared our interior life to healthy or unhealthy fruit. He said, *"Even so, every good tree bears good fruit, but a bad tree bears bad fruit."*[58] It's the inner person that matters to God.

Fruit can look good on the outside even when the interior has significant problems. How often have you bitten into a piece of fruit that looked good on the outside only to be surprised by what you found on the inside? Too often, we judge others by their "put together" exterior without even taking a peek at their interior. And too often, we present our "put together" exterior when we need some interior renewal. Jesus said, *"Whoever hears these sayings of Mine, and does them..."*[59] It is in the outworking of the heart that true interior fruit is revealed. What does good spiritual fruit look like? Jesus gives us a pretty good list in Matthew chapter five. With this list, you can monitor your journey and accurately know others.

Look for...

- A contrite spirit before God (verse 3).
- A spirit broken over the condition of its own heart (verse 4).
- A spirit willing to step aside for the good of others (verse 5).
- A spirit that craves to reveal the character and nature of God (verse 6).
- A spirit of mercy meeting the mercy needs of others (verse 7)

- A pure and unadulterated spirit in its relationship with God (verse 8).
- A spirit of reconciliation, working toward restoration with God and others (verse 9).
- A spirit that is willing and ready to embrace what it does not necessarily desire (verse 10).
- A spirit that receives from God in a way that is instructive to others (verses 7 to 20).
- A spirit that creates ways for authentic reconciliation rather than using anger, vengeance, or judgment (verses 21 to 26).
- A spirit so in love with God that the love destroys and interrupts lust (verses 31 and 32).
- A spirit that is not seeking its justified end but offering an honest answer instead (verses 33 to 37).
- A spirit that is defined by an "extra mile" attitude when misused by others (verses 38 to 48).

Dare to live like a blind man running by living your life to honor God and to serve others.

A CLOSING PRAYER

Father God, You knit together the universe and all that is in it.

You alone are its source and sustainer.

You know us completely; nothing is hidden from You.

Our every motive and hidden thought are visible and laid bare before You, and You are fully acquainted with all our brokenness.

Yet You love us with a love that was costly to You alone.

Bless Your Holy Name!

Our desire is to abandon ourselves to You, Lord.

We hunger and thirst for Your presence, while our highest dream is to know You intimately. Increase our craving for You!

As we know You more intimately, manifest Your presence in us and through us as we give ourselves over to Your leading day by day.

Give us eyes to see Your movement and ears to hear Your gentle words of grace and mercy.

Teach us, O Father, to love others as You have loved us. Increase our capacity to give away that same mercy and grace.

Amen and amen!

ABOUT THE AUTHOR

Chris Conrad has spent his life in service to others as a pastor, fire chaplain, and hospice chaplain. He was called into ministry at the age of thirty-five, and his pastoral ministry has spanned thirty-seven years in various assignments across Arizona, Colorado, California, and Oregon. Chris continues to serve others as a leadership/life coach and is now fulfilling his dream of writing books that inspire people to draw closer to God in Jesus Christ.

An avid family man married for more than fifty years, Chris and his wife, Vickie, live in Arizona with their two daughters, four granddaughters, and one grand-Goldendoodle. One of his favorite activities is spending time, one-on-one, with each of his grandchildren…you should know that they all share a love for donuts. Chris' love for the outdoors has kept him active as a lifelong hiker and backpacker, covering trails in many of the western states, including Alaska, but these days, he most enjoys traveling in his RV with his family and friends. Chris has had many interests across the years, but these days, he is deeply passionate about his fountain pen collection and even repairing an antique pen now and then. A warning here: If you start asking Chris fountain pen questions, you may be stuck in that conversation for a while. Just saying…

For more information about Chris, visit https://www.atthesummitaz.com.

BIBLIOGRAPHY

Bailey, Kenneth E. 2008. *Jesus Through Middle Eastern Eyes*. Downers Grove Illinois: InterVarsity Press.

Barclay, William. 1956. *The Daily Study Bible*. Philadelphia: The Westminster Press.

Filder, Marianne. 2022. *Breaking the Cycles of Bondage*: Unlock Your Destiny. Phoenix Arizona: Bondage Breaking Publishing.

Foster, Richard J. 1998. *Celebration of Discipline: The Path to Spiritual Growth*. San Francisco.

Fry, Steve. 2000. *I Am: The Unveiling of God*. Sisters Oregon: Multnomah Publishers.

Fry, Steven. 2002. *Rekindled Flame: The Passionate Pursuit of God*. Sisters Oregon: Multnomah Publishers.

Hendricks, Howard G. 1991. *Living by the Book*. Chicago, Illinois, Moody Press.

Henry, Matthew. 1721. *Matthew Henry's Commentary on the Whole Bible*. Old Tappen, New Jersey: Fleming H. Revell Company.

Keller, Timothy 2008. *The Reason for God: Belief in an Age of Skepticism*. New York, New York: Penguin Books.

Keller, Timothy 2013. *Walking With God Through Pain and*

Suffering. New York, New York: Penguin Books.

Lockyer, Herbert 1961. *All The Miracles of the Bible*. Grand Rapids, Michigan: Zondervan Publishing House.

MacDonald, George, *The Problem of Pain*.

McManus, Erwin Raphael. 2002. *Seizing Your Divine Moment*. Nashville, Tennessee: Thomas Nelson.

Overman, Christian. 1996. *Assumptions That Affect Our Lives*. Chatsworth, California: Micha 6:8.

Richards, Lawrence O. 1988. *The Teacher's Commentary*. Wheaton Illinois: Victor Books.

Robertson, Archibald Thomas. 1930. *Word Pictures or the New Testament*. Nashville, TN.: Broadman Press.

Stedman, Ray C. 2007. *Let God be God: Life-Changing Truths from the Book of Job*. Grand Rapids, Michigan: Discovery House Publishers.

Tozer, A. W. 1961. *Knowledge of the Holy*. New York, New York: Harper Collins Publishing.

Tozer, A. W. 1993. *The Pursuit of God*. Camp Hill, Pennsylvania: Christian Publication.

Tripp, Paul David. War of Words: *Getting to the heart of your communication struggles*. Phillipsburg, New Jersey: P&R Publishing.

- BIBLIOGRAPHY -

Tripp, Paul David. *Whiter than Snow*. Wheaton, Illinois: Crossway.

Wiersbe, Warren W. 2007. *The Wiersbe Bible Study Commentary*. Colorado Springs Co.: David C. Cook.

REFERENCES

1. Philippians 1:21–23 (ESV)
2. Psalm 51:12
3. John 1:14
4. Isaiah 55:1–3 (NKJV)
5. Psalm 42:1–2 (NKJV)
6. Exodus 33:10–11 (ESV)
7. Foster, Richard J., *Celebration of Discipline*, HarperSanFrancisco, page 1.
8. Psalm 51:10b
9. Exodus 9:16
10. Mark 10:46a (ESV)
11. Mark 10:46a (ESV)
12. John 21:25 (ESV)
13. Exodus 34:6–7a (ESV)
14. Mark 10:46a (ESV)
15. Ephesians 1:9–10 (ESV)
16. Psalm 74:9–10 (ESV)
17. Mark 10:51
18. Bailey, Kenneth E., *Jesus Through Middle Eastern*

Eyes, page 173.

19	Joshua 24:15 (ESV)
	Hebrews 4:16 (ESV)
20	Irwin McManus
21	Mark 10:47–48 (ESV)
22	Mark 10:49–50 (ESV)
23	Psalm 103:14
24	Psalm 139:5 (ESV)
25	Psalm 139:3–6
26	Mark 10:51 (ESV)
27	Matthew 6:21
28	Romans 7:24b (ESV)
29	Romans 7:21–24 (ESV)
30	1 Corinthians 13:5
31	Isaiah 9:2 (ESV)
32	Mark 10:52
33	1 Peter 1:13 (ESV)
34	Matthew 7:21–23 (ESV)
35	Hebrews 2:1–3 (ESV)
36	Revelation 2:4–5 (ESV)

37	Psalm 34:8
38	Isaiah 45:19 (ESV)
39	John 5:17 (ESV)
40	Hebrews 4:12 (ESV)
41	Mark 10:52
42	Mark 10:52
43	MacDonald, George, *The Problem of Pain.*
44	John 9:2
45	1 Peter 4:12 (ESV)
46	Ephesians 4:30 (ESV)
47	1 Thessalonians 5:19 (ESV)
48	John 15:20–21 (ESV)
49	1 Samuel 30:6 (ESV)
50	Exodus 34:6–7 (ESV)
51	Jeremiah 29:13–14 (ESV)
52	Hebrews 11:6 (ESV)
53	Revelation 4:8 (ESV)
54	Hebrews 4:16 (ESV)
55	Psalm 103
56	Ephesians 3:17–19 (ESV)

57   Colossians 1:9–11 (ESV)

58   Matthew 7:24 (NKJV)

59   Matthew 7:24a (NKJV)

Printed in the USA
CPSIA information can be obtained
at www.ICGtesting.com
CBHW071743020724
11025CB00006B/121